Joseph Janvier Woodward

The hospital steward's manual

For the instruction of hospital stewards, wardmasters etc.

Joseph Janvier Woodward

The hospital steward's manual
For the instruction of hospital stewards, wardmasters etc.

ISBN/EAN: 9783337041861

Printed in Europe, USA, Canada, Australia, Japan

Cover: Foto ©ninafisch / pixelio.de

More available books at **www.hansebooks.com**

THE

HOSPITAL STEWARD'S

MANUAL:

FOR THE INSTRUCTION OF

HOSPITAL STEWARDS, WARD-MASTERS, AND ATTENDANTS, IN THEIR SEVERAL DUTIES.

PREPARED IN STRICT ACCORDANCE WITH EXISTING REGULATIONS
AND THE CUSTOMS OF SERVICE IN THE ARMIES OF THE
UNITED STATES OF AMERICA,

AND RENDERED AUTHORITATIVE BY ORDER OF THE SURGEON-GENERAL.

BY

JOSEPH JANVIER WOODWARD, M.D.
ASSISTANT SURGEON U.S.A., MEMBER OF THE ACADEMY OF NATURAL SCIENCES
OF PHILADELPHIA, ETC.

PHILADELPHIA:
J. B. LIPPINCOTT & CO.
1862.

PREFACE.

THE preparation of this little work was suggested to the author by the Surgeon-General. It was hastily written to supply an existing want. Had it been otherwise, more time would have been given to its composition, and perhaps a more complete work would have been the result. It is hoped, however, that it will prove useful to surgeons as well as attendants, and that it will be found a material aid in the laborious duties of the Medical Staff in hospitals and in the field.

J. J. WOODWARD,
Assistant Surgeon U.S.A.

WASHINGTON, Sept. 10, 1862.

OFFICIAL ORDERS.

SURGEON-GENERAL'S OFFICE,
WASHINGTON CITY, August 5, 1862.

Surgeons J. K. Barnes and J. R. Smith, U.S. Army, are hereby appointed a Board to examine and report upon a work entitled "The Hospital Steward's Manual," presented by Assistant Surgeon J. J. Woodward, U. S. Army.

WILLIAM A. HAMMOND,
Surgeon-General U.S.A.

SURGEON-GENERAL'S OFFICE,
WASHINGTON CITY, August 19, 1862.

The Board having critically examined the work presented by Assistant Surgeon J. J. Woodward, U.S.A., entitled "The Hospital Steward's Manual," report that this work is written in strict accordance with the regulations of the army and the customs of the service; that the book supplies a deficiency which has been long felt; and respectfully recommend that it be adopted for the instruction of hospital stewards, and as an authority in all military hospitals in the United States.

JOSEPH K. BARNES,
Surgeon U.S.A.
JOSEPH R. SMITH,
Surgeon U.S.A.

SURGEON-GENERAL'S OFFICE,
WASHINGTON CITY, September 10, 1862.

"The Hospital Steward's Manual," prepared by Assistant Surgeon J. J. Woodward, U.S. Army, having been approved by a Board of Medical Officers, is adopted as a guide to hospital stewards and other attendants, and will be strictly adhered to by them in the discharge of their duties.

WILLIAM A. HAMMOND,
Surgeon-General U.S.A.

CONTENTS.

PART I.—HOSPITAL ATTENDANTS.

PAGE

CHAP. I.—Hospital Stewards.................................. 13

  Sec. 1.—The Rank of Hospital Stewards.................. 13
  " 2.—The Pay of Hospital Stewards....................... 16
  " 3.—The Enlistment and Appointment of Hospital Stewards... 17
  " 4.—The Uniform of Hospital Stewards................. 25

CHAP. II.—Other Hospital Attendants.................... 29

  Sec. 1.—Enlisted Men as Hospital Attendants........ 29
  " 2.—The Hospital Corps..................................... 32
  " 3.—Female Nurses.. 38
  " 4.—Laundresses.. 41

CHAP. III.—General Outline of the Duties of Stewards and other Hospital Attendants............ 42

  Sec. 1.—Number of Stewards and other Attendants allowed in Hospitals and in the Field........ 42
  " 2.—Outline of the Duties of Stewards............... 43
  " 3.—Outline of the Duties of Ward-Masters....... 47
  " 4.—Outline of the Duties of Nurses.................. 54
  " 5.—Cooks and Laundresses............................... 67
  " 6.—Duties of Hospital Attendants in Battle...... 67

CONTENTS.

PART II.—DISCIPLINE, POLICE, AND GENERAL SUPERVISION OF MILITARY HOSPITALS.

                                                                PAGE
CHAP. I.—GENERAL DISCIPLINE OF HOSPITALS............... 77

SEC. 1.—Roll Calls.. 77
" 2.—Daily Order of Hospital Duties..................... 78
" 3.—The Steward's Visits of Inspection.............. 82
" 4.—Sunday Morning Inspection........................ 83
" 5.—Muster of Hospital Attendants and of Soldiers in Hospital absent from their Companies.. 84
" 6.—The Guard.. 92
" 7.—The Guard-House....................................... 93
" 8.—Rules and Regulations for the Government of the Hospital.. 94

CHAP. II.—POLICE AND GENERAL SUPERVISION OF HOSPITALS.. 98

SEC. 1.—The Cleanliness of the Hospital................. 98
" 2.—Ventilation 101
" 3.—Warming.. 105
" 4.—Lighting... 108
" 5.—The Latrine.. 110
" 6.—Baths and Lavatories............................... 112
" 7.—The Wards of the Hospital, their Arrangement and Administration........................ 115
" 8.—The Office of the Hospital........................ 121
" 9.—The Knapsack-Room................................. 127
" 10.—The Laundry.. 129
" 11.—The Linen-Room...................................... 132

CHAP. III.—ADMISSIONS, DISCHARGES, DEATHS, ETC........ 134

SEC. 1.—Admission of Patients............................... 134
" 2.—Return to Duty, Transfer to other Hospitals, Furloughs, Discharges, and Desertions..... 140
" 3.—Of Deaths...'... 143

CONTENTS. 9

PART III.—FOOD AND ITS PREPARATION.

CHAP. I.—Provision Returns, Hospital Stores, Purchases for the Hospital, the Hospital Fund and its Management.................................. 155
 Sec. 1.—Preliminary.. 155
 " 2.—The Ration.. 156
 " 3.—Provision Returns.. 162
 " 4.—Hospital Stores.. 166
 " 5.—Purchases for the Hospital.......................... 166
 " 6.—The Hospital Fund, its Management............. 172
 " 7.—The Care of Provisions and Hospital Stores.. 179

CHAP. II.—Of the Diet-Table 183
 Sec. 1.—Full Diet.. 184
 " 2.—Half Diet... 190
 " 3.—Low Diet... 191
 " 4.—Extra Diet... 192
 " 5.—Specimen of Diet Table............................. 193
 " 6.—Diet Table for Field Hospitals 201

CHAP. III.—Of the Kitchen and its Management.... 203
 Sec. 1.—General Management of the Kitchen 203
 " 2.—Fires and Fuel in General and Post Hospitals 210
 " 3.—Fires and Fuel in Camp Hospitals............. 214

CHAP. IV.—Cooking in Hospitals............................ 219
 Sec. 1.—General Remarks.. 219
 " 2.—Receipts adapted to the Ordinary Diet in Hospitals.. 222
 " 3.—Receipts for Extra Diets............................ 240

PART IV.—THE DISPENSARY.

CHAP. I.—General Arrangement and Management of the Dispensary... 263
 Sec. 1.—Requisitions for Medical Supplies.............. 263

CONTENTS.

Sec. 2.—The Supply Table 267
" 3.—Semi-Annual Returns... 267
" 4.—Arrangement of the Dispensary 270
" 5.—Care of Instruments.. 274

CHAP. II.—HINTS ON PHARMACY FOR HOSPITAL STEWARDS.. 278

Sec. 1.—Remarks on Prescriptions........................... 278
" 2.—Compounding and Distribution of Prescriptions 285

PART V.—HINTS ON MINOR SURGERY AND DRESSINGS FOR HOSPITAL STEWARDS.

CHAP. I.—ON DRESSINGS 297

Sec. 1.—General Preparations for Dressings............ 297
" 2.—On the Dressing of Wounds....................... 299
" 3.—On the Roller Bandage and its Applications 304

CHAP. II.—OPERATIONS IN MINOR SURGERY, PERFORMED BY THE HOSPITAL STEWARD 313

Sec. 1.—Cupping... 313
" 2.—Leeching 317
" 3.—Extraction of Teeth.. 319
" 4.—Injections.. 322

PART I.

HOSPITAL ATTENDANTS.

NOTE.

The hospital attendants authorized by law may be enumerated as follows:—
1. Hospital Stewards.
2. Ward-Masters.
3. Nurses.
4. Female Nurses.
5. Cooks.
6. Laundresses. (Called also Matrons in "Army Regulations.")

Each of these classes will be made the subject of separate remark.

THE

HOSPITAL STEWARD'S MANUAL.

CHAPTER I.

Hospital Stewards.

SECTION I.—THE RANK OF HOSPITAL STEWARDS.

THE hospital steward is a *non-commissioned officer;* he ranks with ordnance sergeants, and next above the first sergeant of a company.* He is therefore entitled by his rank to obedience from all enlisted men who may be in the hospital, whether patients, ward-masters, nurses, or employés, who must cheerfully and promptly comply with all his reasonable and lawful commands. In his relations to the medical officers, or to commissioned officers generally, however, he must never forget that he is an enlisted man, and owes prompt and ready obedience to the lawful commands of his military superiors.

---

* Revised Regulations for the Army, 1861, Art. II, § 4.

In all matters pertaining to discipline, the military laws applying to the hospital steward are the same as for any other soldier, and he is bound, to the same extent, to comply with army regulations, and with the articles of war.

For disobedience of orders, neglect of duty, drunkenness, or any other military offence, the hospital steward may be placed in arrest by the commanding officer, or other competent authority, and may be tried and punished by court-martial, as in the case of other enlisted men. A single exception in favor of the hospital steward is intended especially for the protection of those who originally enlisted as such. It is laid down in the following regulation:—

"The jurisdiction and authority of courts-martial are the same with reference to hospital stewards as in the cases of other enlisted men. When, however, a hospital steward is sentenced by an inferior court to be reduced to the ranks,* such sentence, though it may be approved by the reviewing officer, will not be carried into effect until the case has been referred to the Secretary of War for final action. In these

---

* That is, the rank of a private soldier.

cases of reduction, the application of the man for discharge from service, though not recognized as of right, will generally be regarded with favor, if his offence has not been of too serious a nature, and especially when he has not been recently promoted from the ranks."* It is, however, provided that hospital stewards are not to be tried by regimental or garrison courts-martial, unless by special permission of the department commander.†

Where several hospital stewards are serving together, as frequently happens in the great general hospitals, their relative rank is decided by the seniority of their warrants, as in the case of other non-commissioned officers. This, however, is not construed to prevent the surgeon in charge from selecting the hospital steward regarded by him as the most active and efficient for the position of chief steward, and confiding to his charge the general care of the hospital. The chief steward is *ex officio* the ranking steward for the time-being, and must be obeyed and respected accordingly by the other stewards, as well as by the ward-masters, nurses, and patients.

---

* Revised Regulations, 1861, Art. XLIV. § 1292.
† Revised Regulations, Art. XXXVIII. § 895.

16   THE HOSPITAL STEWARD'S MANUAL.

SECTION II.—THE PAY OF HOSPITAL STEWARDS.

The pay of a hospital steward appointed by the Secretary of War was formerly that of an ordnance sergeant, $22 a month, with one ration a day, and the clothing allowance of an enlisted man. By an act of Congress of April 16, 1862, entitled "An Act to reorganize and increase the efficiency of the medical department of the army," the pay has, however, been increased from $22 to $30 per month, which is the present rate, the other allowances remaining the same.

In barracks he is entitled to one room as quarters, to half a cord of wood monthly from May 1 to September 30, and one cord for each month from October 1 to April 30. The ration is issued only in kind, and is not commuted in money.

The clothing allowance need not be drawn in full; and any savings in this respect are paid to the steward in the final settlement of his accounts.

Acting hospital stewards (see next section) receive but $20 a month, except when serving at posts of more than four companies, when they receive $22 per month; their rations, clothing, allowances, &c. are the same as stewards regularly appointed.

The steward is paid on a hospital muster roll, on which are paid also the medical cadets, female nurses, matrons, and all soldiers in hospital, sick or on duty, who are detached from their companies.

These muster rolls must be made out in the forms furnished from the Adjutant-General's office, and according to the directions expressed on them.*

The surgeon in charge is responsible for the accuracy of the rolls, which must be signed by him and the mustering officer.

Should he re-enlist, the hospital steward is entitled to the same extra pay as other enlisted men. (See next section.)

SECTION III.—OF THE ENLISTMENT AND APPOINTMENT OF HOSPITAL STEWARDS.

Hospital stewards may be appointed from the enlisted men of the army, or may be specially enlisted. The appointment is, in every case, made by the Secretary of War.

---

* See Hospital Muster Roll, Part II. chap. II. § 8.

Non-commissioned officers or soldiers may be appointed hospital stewards, on the recommendation of the senior medical officer of the hospital, post, or command. This recommendation must be endorsed by the company commander, and the commanding officer of the post or detachment, and forwarded by the latter to the Adjutant-General of the army.

"As the object of these more permanent appointments is to procure the services of a more competent body of hospital stewards, no soldier, nor citizen, must henceforth be recommended for appointment, who is not *known* to be temperate, honest, and in every way reliable, as well as sufficiently intelligent, and skilled in pharmacy, for the proper discharge of the responsible duties likely to be devolved upon him."*

· Hospital stewards may also be enlisted, as such, from civil life. Applications, in the handwriting of the candidate, should be addressed to the Surgeon-General, accompanied by testimonials as to character and competency. The enlistment is for the term of three years.

At the expiration of his enlistment, should

---
* Revised Regulations, Art. XLIV. ? 1288.

he desire it, the hospital steward may be re-enlisted by the commanding officer, on the recommendation of the medical officer. He is then entitled, as are all enlisted men on re-enlisting, to $2 per month additional pay, and $1 per month for each subsequent period of five years' service, provided he re-enlists within one month after the expiration of his term of service. When enlisted men are appointed hospital stewards, the appointment is for the remaining unexpired term of service. When enlisted men of the volunteer service are appointed hospital stewards in the regular army, they must first be discharged from service.

In addition, it is provided, to meet the current wants of the service, and especially of troops in the field or distant posts, that the commanding officer may, on the recommendation of the medical officer, detail a soldier to act as temporary steward.

These temporary stewards are generally designated as Acting Hospital Stewards. At posts of more than four companies they receive $22 per month and the allowances of hospital steward; with smaller bodies of troops, the pay and allowances of a sergeant of infantry.*

---

* $20 per month. See act July 5, 1838, sec. 12.

These temporary appointments may be regarded as "affording the means of a careful probation of all soldiers so detailed, who are ambitious of one day deserving a permanent appointment."*

The candidate for enlistment or appointment as hospital steward should be not less than eighteen nor more than thirty-five years of age. He must be able-bodied and free from disease. Previous to his enlistment he is inspected by a medical officer, in the same manner as any other recruit, and will be rejected if found laboring under any disease or disability which would reject a recruit. He should be of honest and upright character, of temperate habits, and good general intelligence. He must have a competent knowledge of the English language, and be able to write legibly and spell correctly. This point must be satisfactorily ascertained before he can be enlisted, as without this qualification it will be impossible for him to keep the books and records, or to attend to the general business of the hospital. In addition, he must have sufficient practical knowledge of pharmacy to enable him to take exclusive charge of the

---

* Revised Regulations, Art. XLIV. § 1289, note.

dispensary, must be practically acquainted with such points of minor surgery as the application of bandages and dressings, the extraction of teeth, and the application of cups and leeches, and must have such knowledge of cooking as will enable him to superintend efficiently this important branch of hospital service.

He should be industrious, temperate, patient, and good-tempered, and actuated by an honorable desire to minister to the extent of his ability to the necessities and comforts of the sick and wounded soldiers who are placed under his charge.

On receiving his appointment, the hospital steward receives, from the office of the Adjutant-General, a warrant made out in the following form :

HOSPITAL STEWARD AT ———.

To all who shall see these presents, greeting:

Know ye, that this is to certify that ——— ———, of the ——— Regiment of ———, having been recommended as a fit person to receive the appointment of *Hospital Steward*, the *Secretary of War* has selected him, in conformity with the second section of the Act of the 16th of August, eighteen hundred and fifty-six, entitled "An Act providing for a necessary increase and better organization of the Medical and Hospital Department of the Army:" And he is *hereby appointed* accordingly, with all the rights, privileges, immunities, and allowances appertaining to said appointment, and with the rank of a sergeant of ordnance. He is, therefore, strictly charged carefully and diligently to perform and execute all duties belonging to said appointment, in conformity with the rules and regulations of the service. And he is to be respected accordingly.
 Given at the ——— ———, City of Washington, this ——— day of ———, 18———.

By command,

THE HOSPITAL STEWARD'S MANUAL. 23

"The accounts of pay, clothing, &c., of hospital stewards must be kept by the medical officers under whose immediate direction they are serving, who are also responsible for certified statements of such accounts, and correct descriptive lists of such stewards, to accompany them in case of transfer; as also that their final statements and certificate of discharge are accurately made out, when they are at length discharged from the service."*

The following is the form of the descriptive roll and account of pay and clothing:—

---

* Revised Reg., Art. XLIV. ? 1293.

24 THE HOSPITAL STEWARD'S MANUAL.

Muster and Descriptive Roll, and Account of Pay and Clothing of ———

No.	Names.	Rank.	DESCRIPTION.					WHERE BORN.		Occupation.	ENLISTED.				LAST PAID.				BOUNTY		Remarks.
			Age.	Eyes.	Hair.	Com-plexion.	Feet.	Inches.	State or Kingdom.	Town or County.		When.	Where.	By whom.	Period.	By Pay-master.	To what time.	Paid, $	Due, $	

	Names.	Wool overalls.	Cotton overalls.	Wool Jackets.	Cotton shirts.	Flannel shirts.	Boots.	Stockings.	Blankets.	Forage-caps.	Great-coats.	(treat-coat) straps.	Leather stocks.	Drawers.	Date of Issue.	By whom Issued.

I certify that the above is a correct transcript from the records of this office. ———

SECTION IV.—OF THE UNIFORM OF HOSPITAL STEWARDS.

The hospital steward should always wear his undress uniform in the hospital, except on those occasions, such as musters and inspections, on which it is necessary for him to appear in full dress. This point is of more importance than at first sight appears. The strictest military discipline is absolutely necessary in a military hospital; and it will be too generally found that an unmilitary neglect of regulations in regard to dress coexists with a general neglect of discipline and regulation in regard to other duties.

The uniform of the hospital steward "*for fatigue purposes,*" that is, for all ordinary duties, consists of the blouse, or sack-coat, and trousers, prescribed by regulations for all foot soldiers. The trousers are to have upon the outer seam of each leg a stripe of crimson worsted lace, one and one-half inch wide. It is advisable that the half chevron described for the full uniform of the hospital steward should also be worn upon the undress coat. He should take enough pride in his personal appearance to keep his clothes neat and his boots clean and well blacked.

The undress cap is the regulation forage cap, similar to that of other enlisted men.

The full uniform of a hospital steward consists of—

1. *Uniform coat*, which is a dark-blue cloth single-breasted frock, the same as that prescribed by army regulations for all enlisted *foot* men; except that the cord or welt of cloth which edges the cuffs and collar is *crimson*, instead of being sky-blue as for infantry, or yellow as for engineers.

2. *Trousers* of dark-blue cloth, with a stripe of crimson lace one and one-half inch wide down and over the outer seam.

3. *Hat*, a black felt hat, the same as that of all enlisted men. The cord of buff and green mixed, the wreath in front of brass, with the letters U. S. in Roman, of white metal. Brim to be looped up to side of hat with a brass eagle, having a hook attached to the bottom to secure the brim. The feather to be worn on the side opposite the loop.

3. *Cravat or stock*, black leather, the same as that of all enlisted men.

4. *Boots or shoes*, the same issued to all enlisted men.

5. *Sash*, "red worsted sash, with worsted bullion fringe ends; to go twice around the waist, and to tie behind the left hip, pendent part not to extend more than eighteen inches below the tie."

6. *Sword belt and plate*, the same as for all non-commissioned officers.

7. *Sword*, the same as for non-commissioned officers.

8. *Chevrons*, "a half chevron of the following description, viz.: of emerald-green cloth, one and three-fourths inches wide, running obliquely downward from the outer to the inner seam of the sleeve, and at an angle of about thirty degrees with a horizontal, parallel to and one-eighth of an inch distant from both the upper and lower edge, an embroidery of yellow silk one-eighth of an inch wide, and in the centre a 'caduceus' two inches long, embroidered also with yellow silk, the head towards the outer seam of the sleeve."*

To indicate service, the additional half chevrons allowed for all non-commissioned

---

* Revised Reg., Art. LI. ₴ 1553.

officers, viz., at the expiration of five years' service, a diagonal half chevron one-half an inch wide, to be worn upon both sleeves of the uniform coat, below the elbow, extending from seam to seam, the front end nearest the cuff, and one-half an inch above the point of the cuff, to be of the same color as the edging on the coat (crimson). In like manner, an additional half chevron, above and parallel to the first, for every subsequent five years of faithful service. Distance between each chevron, one-fourth of an inch.

Overcoat, the same as for enlisted men.

Gloves.—On full-dress occasions, white cotton gloves should be worn.

Scales.—On each shoulder of the uniform coat is worn a metallic *scale*, the same as worn by all non-commissioned officers and enlisted men.

CHAPTER II.

Other Hospital Attendants.

BESIDES the stewards, the following classes of hospital attendants may be enumerated: enlisted men, civilians, the hospital corps, female nurses, and laundresses (matrons of army regulations).

The male attendants were formerly all enlisted men, detailed for the duty by the commanding officer on the recommendation of the surgeon.

Recently, however, the Secretary of War has authorized the employment in certain cases of civilians as cooks and nurses, in general hospitals only; and thus a new body of hospital attendants has been created, which is designated the "Hospital Corps."

SECTION I.—OF ENLISTED MEN AS HOSPITAL ATTENDANTS.

Enlisted men selected as hospital attendants may be either non-commissioned officers or private soldiers. It is usual for non-commissioned officers to be employed as ward-masters, or in some similar responsible positions, only, and private soldiers for all other duty.

In either case, the enlisted man, besides his ordinary pay and emoluments, is entitled to twenty-five cents daily "extra duty pay," which is paid by the paymaster on a roll made out by the surgeon, after the form on p. 31.

The pay and emoluments of these enlisted men as soldiers are obtained from the paymaster, on their descriptive lists, or on the hospital muster roll, duly made out by the surgeon, on forms furnished from the Adjutant General's office.*

The distribution of these attendants as cooks, nurses, &c., and the assignment to each of his duties, is made by the surgeon.

Enlisted men thus employed are under the orders of the surgeon, to whom they are to look up as their commanding officer. They are also under the orders of the hospital steward, to all whose lawful commands they must yield prompt obedience. They are exempt from all other duty, but "shall attend the parades for muster and weekly inspections

---

* See Part II. Chap. I. Sect. 5.

THE HOSPITAL STEWARD'S MANUAL. 31

Roll of Soldiers employed on extra duty as Cooks and Nurses in the Hospital at ———, during the month of ———, 186—, by ———, Surgeon.

No.	Names.	Rank or designation.	Company.	Regiment.	By whose order employed.	Nature of service.	Term of service.			Rate of pay or compensation.			How employed.
							From.	To.	No. of days.	Per diem.			Remarks.
										Dolls.	Cts.	

I certify that the above is a correct roll of the enlisted men employed on extra duty, under my direction, during the month of ———, 186—, and that the remarks opposite their names are accurate and just.

————, Surgeon.

Examined:

————, Commanding.

of their companies at the post, unless specially excused by the commanding officer."*

Sobriety, intelligence, and cheerful obedience to all lawful commands are indispensable qualifications for hospital attendants, and those who show capacity and industry are generally selected by the surgeon for promotion to the higher grades of ward-master and steward.

SECTION II.—OF THE HOSPITAL CORPS.

Civilians may be employed as hospital attendants by the Surgeon-General, and by such surgeons as have received from him the necessary authority. Their pay, emoluments, and the regulations adopted with regard to them are duly set forth in the following circular issued by the Surgeon-General on the subject:—

CIRCULAR No. 4.

SURGEON-GENERAL'S OFFICE, June 5, 1862.

The Secretary of War having authorized in certain cases the employment of civilians as cooks and nurses for duty in general hospitals, (only,) the following rules and instructions are published for the information of all concerned:

---

* Revised Reg., Art. XLIV. § 1257.

Regulations for the Hospital Corps of the United States Army.

The men of the hospital corps will each receive $20 50 per month, besides clothing, rations, and medical attendance.

They will be under military discipline, and subject only to the orders of the medical authorities, and will wear the undress uniform of a private soldier, with a green half chevron on the left fore-arm.

Their duties will be either nursing the sick and wounded of the army in hospitals, cooking, or any other duties with the sick, at the discretion of the medical officers.

They will be divided into squads of eleven, one of whom will be responsible for the efficiency of the rest. One squad will be allowed to every one hundred patients.

At the usual roll-calls, the chief of the squad will answer for the rest to the hospital steward, who will thus learn the number of vacant beds in each ward, and all other particulars concerning the condition and wants of the hospital, which he will report to the medical "officer of the day." The term of the service of the hospital corps will be according to the necessities of the service, or during good conduct.

The amount of pay and clothing received by each nurse, with date, will be recorded on their contract, which will be as a descriptive list to go with the nurse.

The senior medical officer in charge will make a monthly pay-roll of the hospital corps similar to Form 12, Medical Regulations, except the rank and designation, and transmit the same for payment to the nearest medical disbursing officer.

Surgeons in charge of general hospitals. when so authorized, may make contracts with persons for such service according to the provisions set forth herein.

WILLIAM A. HAMMOND,
Surgeon-General.

NOTE.—It is hereby enjoined upon all medical officers that they shall not avail themselves of this special authority of the War Department without first receiving permission of the Surgeon-General to do so, on making a full statement of the facts in the case, and clearly setting forth the reasons why the permission should be granted, except in cases of immediate necessity and urgency, and then the commanding officer must approve. In such exceptional cases the facts will be promptly reported to the Surgeon-General with the necessary explanations, together with a request that permission be given to continue the employment if the necessity still exists.

Civilians employed should possess the physical qualifications necessary for recruits. They should be of good general intelligence, temperate and industrious habits, and should be fully imbued with the idea of the importance of their calling, and of the responsibility of the duties which they assume.

The same strict obedience is exacted from them as from enlisted men.

Civilians employed as nurses or cooks are contracted with by the officer employing them, in accordance with the following form:—

Form of Contract with a Civilian, to act as Hospital Attendant.

I, —— ——, hereby agree to serve in the army of the United States, in the capacity of nurse, and to perform such other duties in connection with the sick and wounded of the army as may be required of me by the medical authorities, and to obey all orders emanating from them; said service to continue for the period of one year, unless sooner discharged; and I will accept, in payment for said service, $20 50, besides clothing, rations, and medical attendance, for each and every month I shall continue to perform the services above stated; and I further agree that $2 shall be retained from my monthly pay till this contract ceases.

————— —————. [SEAL.]

Signed, sealed, and delivered }
    in presence of

————— —————. [SEAL.]

They are paid by a medical disbursing officer, on a roll made out by the surgeon, in the same form as that for enlisted men,[*] except that the columns for rank, regiment, and company are omitted. The following is the form employed:—

---

[*] See sect. 1 of this chapter.

THE HOSPITAL STEWARD'S MANUAL.   37

Roll of Men of the Hospital Corps of the U.S. Army employed in the General Hospital at ———, during the month of ———, 186—.

No.	Name.	By whose order employed.	Nature of service.	Term of service.			Rate of pay or compensation.		We the subscribers do hereby acknowledge to have received of Surgeon ———, at ———, the sums set opposite our respective names, being in full of our pay for the period herein expressed, having signed duplicates hereof,—viz.:		
				From.	To.	No. of days.	Per diem.		Signer's name.	Witness.	Remarks.
							Dolls.	Cts.			

I certify that the above is a correct roll of the hospital corps employed under my direction, during the month of ———, and that the sum set opposite their names is accurate and just.

——— ———, Surgeon.

(Duplicate.)

SECTION III.—OF FEMALE NURSES.

Female nurses are employed in general hospitals, at the discretion of the surgeon in charge, or of the Surgeon-General. Their pay is 40 cents and one ration daily, with quarters and fuel. The ration may be either commuted or drawn in kind.

They are paid on the hospital muster roll, with the stewards, cadets, &c.*

It will generally be found convenient, where female nurses are employed, for the surgeon to appoint the most intelligent and reliable to be the *directress of female nurses*, whose duty it shall be to supervise, to oversee the washing and the distribution of clean clothes, the linen-room and its appurtenances, the issue of delicacies for the sick, and the extra-diet kitchen for their preparation.

In the performance of these duties, she should heartily co-operate with the steward, and strictly obey the orders of the medical officers.

The remaining female nurses will in every case have their special duties designated,

---

* See Hospital Muster Roll.

through the directress, by the surgeon in charge; they may be conveniently assigned to the care of the cleanliness of patients as to dress and person, the supervision, preparation, and administration of extra diets and beverages, and such watching and other care of the sick as the medical officers may direct. In addition, one or more nurses may be employed in the linen-room, in mending and taking care of clothing, &c. &c.

Women employed in this capacity should be intelligent, industrious, and of irreproachable character. They should have a just appreciation of the importance of their duties, and should devote themselves heartily to their proper performance.

During the present war, great exertions have been made to supply female nurses of the proper character to military hospitals, by Miss D. L. Dix, so well known for her philanthropic endeavors to ameliorate the condition of the insane. Miss Dix has been authorized by the War Department to employ female nurses for army hospitals; and, as it is impossible for her to supervise in person all the hospitals, she is authorized to delegate her authority to subordinate agents, not to exceed one for each city or military district. Women wishing employment as nurses must apply to Miss Dix, or to her authorized agents, and medical officers requiring women nurses are directed by the Surgeon-General to apply to Miss Dix, or to her authorized agent for the place where their hospitals are located.

Exception is made to this rule only in cases of urgent need.

Female nurses thus employed may be discharged by the medical officer in charge of the hospital to which they are assigned, if found incompetent, insubordinate, or otherwise unfit for their vocation.*

Besides the nurses furnished by Miss Dix, Sisters of Charity, and the members of other religious orders, have largely volunteered for the duty of nurses during the present war, and, by their devotion, strict obedience to directions, and irreproachable lives, have proved of the greatest service to those hospitals which have been fortunate enough to secure their services. They can be employed only under special instructions from the Surgeon-General's office.

---

* See Circular No. 7, Surgeon-General's Office, Washington, D.C., July 14, 1862.

SECTION IV.—OF LAUNDRESSES.

The laundresses for the hospital (matrons of army regulations) are employed by the surgeon at the rate of one to every twenty patients.

Their pay is six dollars a month, with one ration per day.

They are paid on the hospital muster roll. (F. 2.) Soldiers' wives are selected for this duty wherever practicable. Where the laundresses come to the hospital to wash, the hours of work are regulated by the surgeon; where the clothes are given out to wash, the time allowed for their completion is regulated by the same authority.

CHAPTER III.

General Outline of the Duties of Stewards and other Hospital Attendants.

SECTION I.—NUMBER OF STEWARDS AND OTHER HOSPITAL ATTENDANTS ALLOWED IN HOSPITALS AND IN THE FIELD.

THE number of hospital attendants is fixed by army regulations as follows:

"Ordinarily, hospital attendants are allowed as follows: to a general hospital, one steward, one nurse as ward-master, one nurse to ten patients, one matron to twenty, and one cook to thirty; to a hospital where the command exceeds five companies, one steward and ward-master, one cook, two matrons, and four nurses; to a post or garrison of one company, one steward and ward-master, one nurse, one cook, and one matron, and for every two companies more, one nurse; at arsenals, where the number of enlisted men is not less than fourteen, one matron is allowed.

" The allowance of hospital attendants for troops in the field will be: for one company, one steward, one nurse, and one cook; for each additional company, one nurse; and for commands of over five companies, one additional cook."*

It will be observed that the word *ordinarily* is used in connection with this regulation; and practically, in general hospitals and elsewhere, when any special circumstances render a larger number of attendants necessary, they can generally be obtained by the surgeon on representing the case to the medical director.

Thus, for example, in general hospitals of more than one hundred and fifty patients, more than one hospital steward is usually allowed.

SECTION II.—OUTLINE OF THE DUTIES OF HOSPITAL STEWARDS.

In the field, in post hospitals, and in general hospitals of moderate size, but one steward is generally allowed. His duties embrace all those described in this work as belonging to hospital stewards. He has, under the surgeon, the general supervision of the hospital, regulates its police, discipline,

---

* Revised Reg., Art. XLIV. § 1258.

ventilation, lighting, and warming, attends to the provision returns, carries out the surgeon's instructions as to the management of the hospital fund, makes the purchases for the hospital and takes care of the stores, sees that the cooking is properly executed, the property of the hospital duly cared for, and, in fact, is responsible to the surgeon for the general administration of the institution.

Besides these duties, he takes charge of the dispensary, puts up the prescriptions, and performs all those duties described in the chapter on the dispensary and its management, as well as renders to the surgeon such assistance as may be necessary in dressings and minor surgery.

These duties, however, are so extensive that during the present war it has been found expedient to authorize more than one steward in general hospitals of a hundred and fifty patients or upwards.

Where *two* hospital stewards are thus assigned to a general hospital, one should be put in exclusive charge of the dispensary, and should relieve the other of all except the strictly administrative duties of the house.

Where *three* hospital stewards are assigned

to a general hospital, one should be put in charge of the cooking department. His duty should be to supervise the cooks and all pertaining to the kitchen, to receive and take charge of the provisions when they arrive at the hospital, and be responsible for their economical use. One should have charge of the dispensary, &c., and a third attend to the administrative duties of the house.

Where more than three hospital stewards are allowed, an additional steward may be detailed for the dispensary, another to assist in the administrative duties of the house, and so on.

As a general rule, three hospital stewards will be found quite sufficient for hospitals of five hundred patients.

The hospital steward charged with the administrative duties of the house is designated the chief steward. He receives obedience from all non-commissioned officers, enlisted men, and citizen nurses in the hospital, and is immediately responsible to the surgeon in charge for the performance of his duties.

The details of the several duties of hospital stewards will be found throughout the volume.

In addition to these duties, there is a special duty directed in regulations, to which the attention of hospital stewards is especially called, because of late it has been too much neglected, and great inconvenience has resulted in consequence.

It is provided in regulations that "hospital stewards, whenever stationed in places whence no post return is made to the Adjutant-General's office, or when on furlough, will at the end of every month report themselves by letter to the Adjutant-General and Surgeon-General, as well as to the medical director of the military department in which they may be serving; to each of whom they will *also* report each assignment to duty, or change of station, ordered in their case, noting carefully the number, date, and source of the order directing the same. They will also report monthly when on furlough to the medical officer in charge of the hospital to which they are attached."*

Careful compliance with this regulation will save much inconvenience to the steward, as well as to the authorities. It is the only convenient way of knowing the whereabouts of any individual steward. It is therefore urged upon their attention, not merely as a military duty, but as a matter of convenience to themselves.

---

* Revised Reg., Art. XLIV. ₰ 1292.

SECTION III.—OUTLINE OF THE DUTIES OF THE WARD-MASTER.

The duties of the ward-master are, to a certain extent, described in army regulations, in which it is ordered that the surgeon " will require the ward-master to take charge of the effects of the patients; to register them in a book; to have them numbered and labelled with the patient's name, rank, and company; to receive from the steward the furniture, bedding, cooking-utensils, &c. for use, and keep a record of them, and how distributed to the wards and kitchens; and once a week to take an inventory of the articles in use, and report to him any loss or damage to them, and to return to the steward such as are not required for use."*

It will be seen here that two duties are specially assigned to the ward-master. First, the care of the effects of patients. Second, the care of the hospital furniture and utensils.

In order that the ward-master may take charge of the effects of patients, he has assigned to him the care of the knapsack-room.†

---

* Revised Reg., Art. XLIV. § 1246.
† See Part II. Chap. II. Sec. 9.

On the reception of patients, their effects are at once turned over to the ward-master, excepting only money, watches, or other valuables, which are given to the surgeon for safe keeping.

The ward-master examines them, makes a list on the back of the patient's ticket, and enters all in a book kept for the purpose, in accordance with the form on p. 49.

After entering the list of articles in his book, the ward-master will cause them to be neatly packed in the knapsack, have the overcoat and blankets properly folded and strapped upon it, and affix to the package a label, on which is written the name, rank, and company of the owner, with the number of his ward and bed. It is then to be carried to the knapsack-room and placed upon the appropriate shelf.

Muskets, sabres, pistols, &c. are to be similarly labelled and placed on the arms-rack in the knapsack-room.

When the patient leaves the hospital, his effects are to be duly returned to him, except when he is discharged from service, in which case arms and other United States property are to be retained by the ward-master, the government property thus accumulating in the

Ward-master's Account of Clothing, Arms, Equipments, &c., of Patients in Hospital.

Date.	No.	Names.	Rank.	Regiment or corps.	Company.	Coats.	Jackets.	Overalls.	&c.	Muskets.	Knapsacks.	&c.	&c.	&c.	When delivered.	Remarks.

Remarks will note to whom the articles were delivered, what money, &c., were left by those who die; and to whom they were given.

hospital to be turned over from time to time, on orders received from the surgeon, to the Ordnance department.

When the patient dies in hospital, the ward-master is to furnish the surgeon with a statement of his effects, copied from his account-book, and is to retain them in his possession until he receives orders from the surgeon as to their disposition.*

Where no legal claimant appears for property accumulating, either from deceased or deserted soldiers, or from sources unknown, it is to be retained until orders are received for its disposition from proper authority.

In order that the ward-master may properly care for the hospital furniture for which he is responsible, he must keep a record of it, and of its distribution to the office, wards, kitchen, &c. &c.

This record is kept in accordance with the following form:—

---

* Revised Regulations, Art. XVII.

		Ward-master's Account of Furniture, Cooking-Utensils, Bedding, &c. in use.
	No. of ward or kitchen.	
	Bunks.	
	Bedsacks.	
	Sheets.	
	Blankets.	
	Kettles.	
	Spoons.	
	Knives.	
	Forks.	
	&c.	
	&c.	
	Lost.	
	Worn out.	
	Destroyed by order.	
	Returned to steward.	
The remarks will state how articles have been lost, and by whom destroyed, or the persons suspected, &c.	Remarks.	

The above is the form suggested in regulations. The following form, however, will be adopted as more convenient in large hospitals.

Each page of a small blank-book is to be devoted to a separate ward, kitchen, office, or other apartment, and is to be ruled in accordance with the following form:—

Ward No. ——

Names of articles.	Number.	Lost.	Worn out.	Destroyed by order.	Returned to the steward.	Remarks.
Here enter the names only of articles of furniture actually in the apartment.						The remarks to state how articles have been lost, and by whom destroyed, or the person suspected.

Each page is to be headed with the name of the ward or apartment to which it belongs. In making out the original inventory, or recording the original issues, the names of those articles only are to be entered which are

THE HOSPITAL STEWARD'S MANUAL. 53

actually in the apartment concerned, leaving the rest blank to record subsequent additions.

The chief nurse, cook, or other attendant in charge of a ward or apartment, should be furnished with a copy of the ward-master's inventory for his particular ward. As the ward-master is responsible for the due preservation of *all* the hospital property, so, in like manner, is the chief nurse or other attendant, in charge of a particular apartment, responsible to the ward-master for the articles intrusted to his care, as set forth in the inventory furnished him.

Once every week the ward-master is to go over the hospital with his book, and to compare the list for which each ward, &c. is responsible, with the articles actually present. All articles not needed for current use are to be returned to the steward. Loss or damage is to be duly reported to the surgeon.

In a hospital of considerable size, the ward-master may need assistance in the performance of these duties; in which case, one or more hospital attendants may be designated by the surgeon in charge as assistant ward-masters.

SECTION IV.—OUTLINE OF THE DUTIES OF NURSES.

The duties of nurses are the same, whether they belong to the hospital corps or are enlisted men temporarily detailed for the purpose.

Each ward has its nurses specially assigned to it by the surgeon in charge. One of these is designated by him as the chief nurse, who is held responsible by the ward-master for the care of the furniture, utensils, and other hospital property, and by the steward for the discipline, police, and general administration of the ward.

At the option of the surgeon, a female nurse may be assigned to this duty.

The chief nurse will see that the beds are duly made up in the morning; that chamber-pots, bed-pans, and urinals are emptied whenever used; that the ward is properly swept and cleaned daily; that the meals of those patients who are confined to bed are furnished them at the proper hour; that those patients who go to the common table are assembled at the dinner-hour, to march to the dining-hall; that the medicines are sent for when notification of their readiness is received from the dispensary; that they are administered to the patient; that the ward is properly ventilated, free from all close or unpleasant odors, properly lighted at night, and in the winter-time properly warmed; and that all the police regulations established by the surgeon·in charge are scrupulously complied with. He will maintain order and discipline among the attendants and patients, and report all neglect of duty, disobedience of orders, absentees, &c., to the steward.

He will attend the several roll-calls, and there make to the steward report of the condition of the ward, of absentees, &c.

When the surgeon visits the ward, he will accompany him from bed to bed with a slate or memorandum-book, in which he will note the diet, directions as to the administration of medicine, and other specific directions with regard to each patient; and he will be held responsible that these directions are properly carried out.

These duties are responsible and important, and require sobriety, fidelity, and intelligence on the part of the attendant to whom they are intrusted. Too great care cannot, therefore, be exercised in the selection of the chief nurse, who should be at once degraded by the surgeon if he proves incompetent or negligent.

In small wards of ten or fifteen beds, the chief nurse may, in addition to these duties, assume the care of a share of the patients. In wards of twenty beds and upwards, however, it will be found advisable to assign to him only the general supervision and responsibility above outlined.

The beds in each ward are to be divided equally among the remaining nurses, each of whom is to be responsible for all that pertains to those placed under his charge.

He will see that convalescents who are able make their beds immediately after rising in the morning, and will himself make those beds whose occupants are unable to do so. Where patients are confined to bed, their beds should likewise be carefully made up daily, or oftener when their comfort requires it.

Where the patient is able, he may rise from the bed and sit in a chair, or lie in an adjacent bed, as the case may be, while his bed is being made. But where this is impossible, as in severe cases of fevers, wounds with fractures, &c., the making of the bed becomes a matter of some difficulty as well as of importance. To neglect it, besides rendering the patient uncomfortable, would be to make cleanliness impossible, and to predispose to excoriations and to bed-sores. But caution is necessary in executing the task. The pillow may be removed from under the head, shaken up, the case changed when necessary, and replaced. The bed-covers may be removed, the bottom sheet smoothed, drawn upon first on one side and then on the other, so as to remove wrinkles, all crumbs, &c. which may have accumulated on it brushed away, and then the upper sheet, blankets, and coverlet replaced neatly and rapidly.

Where it is necessary to change the bottom sheet, this may readily be done by pinning the clean sheet to the margin of the dirty one, so that as the one is gently drawn away the other is carried into place. The pins should be placed with their heads towards the direction in which the sheet is to be drawn; otherwise their points are liable to catch in the mattress, or the clothes and flesh of the patient.

In cases of fractures of the lower extremities, and other severe injuries, where harm might result from an incautious movement, this duty should only be performed in the presence of the attending surgeon.

The nurse is also immediately responsible for the personal cleanliness of the patients under his charge. He will see that, when they are able to do so, they wash themselves daily, and change their under-clothes at least once a week. Where the patient is unable to wash himself and change his clothes, these duties must be performed for him by the nurse.

The nurse must therefore daily wash the hands and faces and comb the hair of those patients who are unable to wait on themselves. This duty should be performed gently and thoroughly, and without spilling water upon the bed or floor. Where patients are long confined to bed, as in cases of fractures, the feet, limbs, and body should also be washed from time to time. A sponge will be found useful in these cases, both in applying soap and in subsequently removing it.

General sponging of the body should not, however, be resorted to in fevers or other acute diseases, except with the permission of the surgeon. Where patients are obliged to use the bed-pan, urinal, or chamber-pot or chair, the nurse should furnish it to them on the want being made known, and immediately after it is used carry it out of the ward, empty it, cleanse it, and restore it to its place. On no account should vessels containing excrement or urine be allowed to remain even for a few minutes in the ward.

Attention to this particular is so indispensable in a sanitary point of view, that the chief nurse should hold each nurse strictly responsible for the faithful performance of the duty.

Where, from involuntary evacuations of urine or fæces, the patient soils his clothes or his bed, as frequently happens in low forms of fever, in injuries accompanied by paralysis, &c., they should be immediately changed. For the same reason, a piece of oiled silk, oil-cloth, or gutta-percha cloth, should be introduced between the sheet and the mattress, in cases where such an accident may be anticipated, to protect the mattress from injury.

In suppurating wounds, or in cases where water dressings are applied, a piece of oiled silk or gutta-percha cloth should always be employed to protect the bedclothes.

Bedclothes stained with pus or blood should be immediately changed, and economy is to be consulted by protecting the bedclothes and clothes of the patient from being soiled, and not by retaining foul linen, &c. about him to avoid frequent changes. Absolute cleanliness is indispensable to secure the health of wards.

Another point of importance is, to see that patients are kept free from lice and other vermin. This is, to a great extent, secured by attention to personal cleanliness. But some other points may be mentioned.

Bedbugs are best avoided by cleanliness of the beds, secured by occasional wiping with soap and water, especially in all joints and crevices. They are less likely to be found in iron bedsteads, where the mattress rests on wooden or iron slats, than in wooden cots with sacking-bottoms: where they exist, they may be destroyed by washing the crevices with a solution of corrosive sublimate in alcohol, after destruction of all visible on search.

Lice may be removed by the use of the fine-toothed comb, of strong soap and water, and, where necessary, of weak mercurial ointment, or of ointment or infusion of fish-berries, (*Cocculus indicus*, one drachm of the powder to the ounce of lard, or one ounce to the pint of boiling water.) Infusion or tincture of nux vomica also answers the same purpose.

THE HOSPITAL STEWARD'S MANUAL. 61

These medicinal agents, however, should never be resorted to without the consent of the surgeon; and where infusion of fish-berries, or of nux vomica, is employed, the greatest care should be exercised that it is not accidentally employed internally, as it is a deadly poison.

It is also the duty of the nurse to administer the medicines to the patients, and in other respects to carry out the directions of the surgeon. He should, therefore, with the chief nurse, accompany the surgeon in his visits to the patients under his care, and either himself write upon a slate or in a memorandum-book the surgeon's directions for each, or should have free access to the book of the chief nurse in which this record is made.

The nurse should remember that absolute obedience in these respects is his military duty, and that every time he disobeys or neglects the surgeon's directions as to the care of the patient in any particular, he risks unnecessarily the life of a fellow-creature. It is not for him to judge of the propriety or importance of the measures directed : for this the surgeon is responsible : blind and complete obedience is necessarily required of him, and for this he will be held strictly responsible.

The nurse will also see that those of his patients go to the common table for their meals who are authorized to do so by the surgeon, and these only. He will distribute to the others the diet allowed for each by the surgeon, and, where the patient is unable to feed himself, will with his own hands administer the food in accordance with directions received. The same obedience to the surgeon's orders is required here as in the administration of remedies, and for the same reason. The nurse cannot know in any case how fatal may be the results of neglect or disobedience.

It will be seen that for the proper performance of these duties the nurse should in every case be able to read and write.

In addition to the special duties which each nurse owes to the patients under his charge, there are certain general duties in every ward, which are distributed among the nurses, each of whom is to be held responsible for the due performance of the duties assigned him.

Thus, to one should be assigned the sweeping and cleaning of the floor, walls, and windows, to another the maintenance of the fires and the superintendence and management of the lights, to a third the cleanliness of the bath-room, lavatory, and water-closets attached to the ward, &c.

Two or more nurses are to be detailed daily to carry food from the kitchen to the ward, one or more to bring the medicines from the dispensary to the ward, two or more to relieve each other on duty as night nurses where these are required by the emergency of particular cases or the general directions of the surgeon.

The chief nurse, with the permission of the surgeon, may make this distribution of duty, and should keep in a memorandum-book a list of the attendants under his orders, with the duties assigned to each, in order that no disputes may arise as to who is responsible for any of the business of the ward.

Night nurses may be either the ordinary attendants of the ward detailed in turn for that purpose, or a special set of attendants or night watchers detailed for that duty only.

In a great institution, the latter is the best plan. One night nurse should be assigned to each ward, and one to the general supervision of the whole house, whose duty it shall be to go over the house every hour during the night, inspect the fires and lights, and see that the several night nurses are attending to their duties.

The night nurses go on duty at tattoo, and are relieved at reveille. They have the day to themselves for rest and sleep.

Where there are no special night nurses, the ordinary attendants of the house take turns in performing this duty. For this purpose a roster should be made out by the steward, and each detailed in his turn, with a corresponding period of rest to follow his tour of duty.

Besides the nurses proper, certain attendants may be detailed, at the discretion of the surgeon, for duty in the office, as clerks, &c., as assistants in the dispensary, as assistants to the ward-master, and for such other duties as are not otherwise provided for. Each of these attendants has his special duties specifically assigned him by the surgeon, to whom, as well as to the steward or ward-master under whose orders he may be placed, he is responsible for their proper performance.

A list should be kept in the office of all the attendants in the house, with the duties assigned to each, which may be made out in the following form:—

List of Hospital Attendants.

Name.	Regiment or Corps.	Company.	When appointed.	By whose authority.	Duty.	Remarks.
					Here state the ward or place where on duty, whether as nurse, and in what ward, attendant on office or elsewhere, assistant to ward-master, or in dispensary.	Here mention when relieved from duty, and why, and such other matters as necessary.

From this list a memorandum of hospital attendants may be made up, which should be hung in a conspicuous place in the office, and should be corrected whenever any changes are made.

	Names.
Stewards.	
In office.	
In dispensary.	
In kitchen.	
In knapsack-room.	
Ward 1.	
Ward 2.	
Ward 3.	
&c.	
&c.	
&c	

SECTION V.—DUTIES OF COOKS AND LAUNDRESSES.

The duties of cooks and laundresses will be described in full in the articles on the kitchen and laundry, (*q. v.*)

SECTION VI.—DUTIES OF HOSPITAL ATTENDANTS IN BATTLE.

The duties of the hospital attendants in battle are of the highest importance, and on their faithful execution the successful succoring of the wounded must in a great measure depend. The surgeon must, therefore, exact the strictest discipline during an engagement, and the slightest disobedience of orders or neglect of duty must be punished in an exemplary manner.

The attendants may be divided into two classes: those who remain at the depots established at the rear of the line of battle, and those who go upon the field.

Those who remain at the depots are selected for this purpose by the surgeon in charge of the depot.

One or more experienced stewards, one or more cooks, and a sufficient number of nurses will be detailed for this purpose. The number of attendants needed will vary with the number of surgeons assigned to the depot for duty, and the probable number of wounded: it is in every case determined by the surgeon in charge of the depot.

The depot established, the hospital steward at once proceeds to open such panniers and chests as may be necessary to get out a sufficient number of bandages, dressings, stimulants, and opiates, or other articles required by the surgeons.

If the depot is near the scene of actual conflict, no more should be laid out than is absolutely necessary for actual use, in order that, if it becomes advisable to change the location of the depot, it may be effected with as little loss of time as possible.

Instrument-cases should be laid out and unlocked, but instruments should not be laid out, except by the surgeon, as they are needed for particular operations; and, for the same reasons, so soon as the surgeon is done with any instrument, it should be at once carefully cleaned and replaced in the case.

A house, barn, or other building, is generally selected as a depot, if it is practicable to do so. When this is the case, the attendants should at once be set to work by the steward in cleaning and preparing it for the reception of the wounded. The cooks, meanwhile, should make a fire, and prepare tea and soup for their refreshment.

Water is to be brought, both for drinking purposes and for the surgeons' use. Sponges are to be soaked, and every necessary preparation made.

When the wounded begin to arrive, some of the attendants assist in removing them from the ambulances and carrying them to the places assigned by the surgeon; while others wait on the surgeons during the operations and dressings, and render such assistance as may be required of them.

At the principal depots in the rear, the same preparations are made, but on a larger scale. In every case, the special arrangements are ordered by the medical officers, and the assignments of the several duties to the assistants are made by the same authority.

The hospital attendants who go upon the field may be divided into two classes: those who accompany the medical officers, who go upon the field for the immediate succor of the wounded, and those who accompany the ambulances and litters to help the wounded into them, or bear the hand-stretchers.

Each medical officer should be accompanied upon the field by an orderly, who carries the hospital knapsack, in which is placed a supply of instruments, dressings, &c. for immediate use. When the surgeon stops to give his services to a wounded man, the orderly at once unslings his knapsack and prepares to hand out to the surgeon the articles needed in dressing the patient.

The medical officer should also be accompanied by two intelligent attendants, one of them a hospital steward where possible, to assist him in any operation he may perform upon the field.

The ambulances are to be accompanied by a sufficient number of attendants, with hand-stretchers, to pick up the wounded and carry them from positions inaccessible to the ambulances, or where it is not advisable that these should go, to the nearest ambulances, or field depot.

In lifting the wounded and placing them upon the stretchers, the greatest tenderness should be used, especially where there is reason to believe that bones are fractured. The stretchers are each to be carried by two stout men, who are to take pains to walk so that, while the foremost steps off with his right foot, the other may step off with his left, as by so doing the patient is less likely to be jolted, and the stretcher is tilted less, than where this precaution is neglected. When the patient is to be placed in the ambulance, the attendants carefully place the litter upon the ground, in the rear of the ambulance, draw out the ambulance-litter on which he is to lie, place it by the side of the stretcher, gently transfer him to it, and carefully raise it from the ground and slide it back into its place in the vehicle. At least three men are necessary for this purpose, one on each side of the end of the litter first introduced into the ambulance, and one at the other end. Care should be taken not to tilt the litter, or jar it unnecessarily in getting it into place, and, after having placed it, to secure it so that it cannot slip out in the movements of the vehicle.

The ambulance-driver should keep his horses perfectly quiet while patients are being introduced, and should move carefully, so as to avoid jolting as much as possible while going to the depot.

Arrived at the depot, the ambulance is to be backed up as near the entrance as possible, the litters, with the patients upon them, are to be drawn out one by one, and carried to the place assigned them, the patients removed, the litters replaced, and the ambulance starts off once more for a fresh load.

The number of hospital attendants allowed in the field being usually found insufficient for this purpose, an additional detail is generally required. The musicians are usually selected; but, in addition to these, an adequate number of temporary assistants will generally be furnished by the commanding officer, at the request of the surgeon.

The principle endeavored to be established is that the number of men actually on that duty should be sufficiently large to give all reasonable assistance during the engagement, in order that there may be no excuse for soldiers to leave the ranks under the pretence that they are needed to assist the wounded.

Hospital attendants and soldiers specially detailed to the ambulance corps during an engagement should remember that their duty is strictly a military one, and that there is no more excuse for cowardice or for disobedience of orders in their case than there is in that of any other soldiers on duty on the field of battle.

PART II.

DISCIPLINE, POLICE, AND GENERAL SUPERVISION OF MILITARY HOSPITALS.

CHAPTER I.

The General Discipline in the Hospital.

A MILITARY hospital requires administration according to the strictest military discipline. Nothing short of this will secure efficiency. The surgeon holds the chief steward responsible for the condition of every part of the institution under his charge. The steward, on the other hand, holds his several subordinates responsible for the due performance of their duties. The details of these various duties are found throughout this work: here, therefore, we limit ourselves to certain general regulations which will be found necessary to maintain order.

SECTION I.—OF THE ROLL-CALLS.

A roll-call of all the stewards, ward-masters, nurses, cooks, and other attendants or extra-duty men, should be held at least twice daily, —at reveille and tattoo. A noon roll-call is also desirable. The stewards should be called first, where practicable; the nurses in charge of wards should be called next. Each, as he answers to his name, should report whether all the patients under his care are present or not, —a fact which he must ascertain, by actual inspection, before leaving the ward to go to roll-call. These roll-calls are of great importance in large hospitals: they should, therefore, be strictly regarded as a military duty, and all attendants not present should be punished as absent without leave, unless excused on account of special duty.

SECTION II.—DAILY ORDER OF HOSPITAL DUTIES.

The following schedule will be found convenient for the business of the hospital:—

1. Reveille, at 6½ A.M. in winter, and 5 A.M. in summer. Morning roll-call, fifteen minutes after.
2. Breakfast-call, 7 A.M. in winter, and 6 A.M. in summer.
3. Surgeon's call, 9 A.M. in winter, and 8½ in summer.
4. Dinner, 12 M., preceded by noon roll-call when so ordered.
5. Surgeon's evening call, 5 P.M.

6. Supper, 6 P.M.
7. Tattoo and evening roll-call, 8 P.M.
8. Taps (lights extinguished), 9 P.M.

These calls should, whenever possible, be sounded upon a bugle or beaten on a drum, in order that all patients and attendants may be informed. The hours for each call will, in every case, be regulated by the surgeon in charge.

At reveille, all attendants, and such convalescents as are able to do so, will rise, wash and dress; after which each convalescent patient who is able will make his own bed; the attendants will make theirs, and will immediately proceed each about his several duties, such as sweeping the floors, the passages, &c., cleaning the spittoons, and similar work.

At breakfast-call, those convalescents who are able will go to the dining-hall to breakfast, together with the attendants, except those whose duty it is to attend to the distribution of food to patients confined to bed. This distribution should be made while the convalescents are absent at their breakfast,—the preparations having been previously completed, so that the distribution may commence immediately after they leave the room.

The convalescent patients should not be allowed to straggle irregularly through the house to their breakfast or any of their other meals.

They should be drawn up in order in each ward by the chief nurse, who should call the roll, to see that all those directed by the surgeon to take their meals at the general table are there, and no others; after which they should be marched, by one of the attendants, from the ward, through the passages, to the dining-hall. After breakfast they should be marched back in the same order.

The attendants employed in the distribution of food to patients in bed should receive their breakfast immediately after all the patients have received theirs. The chief nurse of each ward will see that immediately after breakfast the ward is put in order for the visit of the surgeon. No patient should be allowed to leave his ward after breakfast, except for necessary purposes, before the surgeon's visit.

At surgeon's call, the several surgeons proceed at once to visit the wards under their charge, examining each patient carefully, and causing the prescription and diet for each to be entered in the prescription and diet book. The prescription and diet book goes to the steward in charge of the dispensary, who puts up the medicines, attaching to each bottle, box, or package a label, on which is written the number of the ward and bed, the name of the patient, date of the prescription, with the directions as to dose, time of taking, &c.

The chief nurse of each ward should keep a slate, on which he should enter opposite the name of each patient the diet allowed, with any specific directions which may be given by the surgeon in individual instances.

At dinner and supper call, the same general order is to be followed as was described for breakfast-call.

At surgeon's evening call, the regular second visits of the surgeon are made to those patients who require it, in the same manner as in the morning.

At tattoo, all patients must make their preparations for retiring, and all must be in bed at nine o'clock, when taps should be sounded and unnecessary lights extinguished.

SECTION III.—THE STEWARD'S VISITS OF INSPECTION.

Besides the visits which he necessarily pays to different parts of the house in the execution of his several duties, the chief steward should pay every part of the hospital a formal visit twice or three times daily.

The middle of the morning, the middle of the afternoon, and at evening, between taps and tattoo, are good times for these visits. To these may be added a visit about half an hour after taps, to inspect the condition of the lights and fires.

At these regular visits, the steward should note the condition of every thing, and especially the order, the cleanliness, the ventilation, the lighting, and the warming of the building: the state of the kitchen and dining-room, of the bath-rooms and the latrines, is also to be carefully observed. Any negligence or violation of duty must be at once corrected; and whenever repairs are needed or gross violations of discipline have occurred, it should be at once reported to the surgeon in charge.

SECTION IV.—OF SUNDAY MORNING INSPECTIONS.

In post hospitals it is usual for the commanding officer to complete his Sunday morning inspection by inspecting the hospital and its appendages in company with the surgeon. In general hospitals the Sunday morning inspection is usually conducted by the surgeon in charge. The proper time for such inspections is between the hours at which the attending surgeons have completed their visits and dinner-call,—say between ten and twelve o'clock. The steward should go through the hospital immediately before the inspection commences, and see that all things are properly prepared.

To prepare for inspection. The hospital should be neat and clean; those patients who are sitting up should be neatly dressed in uniform, their faces and hands clean, hair neatly brushed, and shoes well blacked. The attendants and stewards should appear in full-dress uniform according to their rank, except where the inspecting officer may previously have ordered that undress uniform only need be employed.

The inspecting officer visits all parts of the

84 THE HOSPITAL STEWARD'S MANUAL.

hospital, the store-rooms, dispensary, kitchen, knapsack-room, bath-rooms, latrines, &c., as well as the several wards.

The steward enters each ward before him and commands *attention*, on which all patients who are able to do so, rise and stand in the position of attention until the inspecting officer has passed out.

SECTION V.—ON THE MUSTER OF HOSPITAL ATTENDANTS AND OF SOLDIERS ABSENT FROM THEIR COMPANIES IN HOSPITAL.

On the last day of the months of February, April, June, August, October, and December, the enlisted hospital attendants and soldiers, both sick and on duty, are mustered for their pay. In the field, and at post hospitals, the mustering officer who musters the troops or garrison to which the hospital is attached performs this duty. In general hospitals it is usually performed by the surgeon in charge.

The muster roll having been previously prepared under the supervision of the steward, the attendants, and the patients who are able to do so, are duly assembled on muster day, and the roll called in the presence of the mustering officer, a mark being put before the name of each individual present. Subsequently the several wards are visited seriatim, and the muster roll completed by checking upon the roll the names of the patients in bed in each.

The form of the muster roll, with the directions for making it out, are given on pp. 86, 87, following.

86   THE HOSPITAL STEWARD'S MANUAL.

Muster Roll of Steward, Ward-Master, Cooks, Nurses, Matrons, and detached Soldiers, sick, in the Hospital of ———, ———, Army of the United States, from the —— day of ——, 18—, when last mustered, to the —— day of ——, 18—.

No.	Names present and absent.	Rank.	Company.	Regiment.	How mustered in the Army.			Enlisted.			Attached to hospital.		Last paid.		Bounty.		Names present.	Remarks. (See p. 88.)
					When.	Where.	By whom.	Period.	When.	How employed.	By pay-master.	To what time.	Paid.	Due.				
													Dolls.	Dolls.				

	Mos.	Period paid for.						Pay Roll of the Hospital from the —— day of ——, 186—, when last paid, to the —— day of ——, 186—.
	Days.							
	Dolls.	Pay per month.						
	Dolls.	Amount of pay.						
	Cts.							
	Dolls.	Retained pay.						
	Cts.							
	Dolls.	Paid.	Bounty.					
	Dolls.	Due.						
		Total amount due.						
		Amount of stoppages.						
		Balance paid.						
		Received payment of.						
		Witness.						

NOTES.

1. Under the head of "Remarks," the *date* of any soldier's *joining*, whether *originally*, or from *any absence;* all changes of rank, by *promotion, appointment,* or *reduction,* with *date* of same, and *No., date,* &c., of order; all *authorized stoppages, fines, sentences,* with *No., date,* &c., of order, &c. : in case of ABSENCE, the *nature* and *commencement* of, *No., date,* &c., of order, and *period* assigned for same (to be *repeated on every roll while it lasts*); if *wounded* in battle, or *injured on duty,*—if *sick* or *confined,* a remark to that effect, &c. &c.,—must be *carefully stated* opposite to the name of the person concerned, *with every thing else necessary, either to account fully* for *every individual,—to guide the paymaster,*—or *insure justice to the soldier and to the United States.*

2. In noting STOPPAGES to be made for *loss* or *damage* to public property, the *gross amount* due for *Ordnance, Horse Equipments, Clothing,* &c., will be *separately* stated in the order enumerated in par. 1187, G. R.

3. Additional pay, due under *Sec. 2, Act of Aug.* 4, 1854, will be thus noted,—viz.: "*For* 1*st re-enlist.* $2 *pr. mo.* ;" or, "*For* 2*d re-enlist.* $3 *pr. mo.* ;" or, "*For* 3*d re-enlist.* $4 *pr. mo.*," &c., &c. That due under *Sec.* 3 *of the same act,* thus: " *For cert. of merit,* $2 *pr. mo.*" That due under *Sec.* 4 *of the same act,* thus: " *In lieu of comm.* $2 *pr. mo.*"

4. The *instalments* of Bounty due, under *Sec.* 3, *Act of June* 17, 1850, are paid as follows : $\frac{1}{10}$, $\frac{1}{8}$, $\frac{1}{5}$, $\frac{1}{4}$, at the end of the 1st, 2d, 3d, and 4th years, respectively, the remainder at the expiration of enlistment ; and will, under the head of "Remarks," be noted thus: "*Ret'd Bounty due,* 1*st* (or 2*d,* 3*d, &c.*) *inst.* $ ——." See G. O. 20 of 1850. *Besides* which, in the columns headed "Bounty Paid" and "Bounty Due," must be entered, in figures, the *whole amount hitherto paid,* and the *whole amount yet due,* on account of said bounty.

5. The "three months' extra pay," for re-enlistment, under Sec. 29, Act of July 5, 1838, being paid by the recruiting officer, should not be noted on the muster rolls.

6. The roll of those *belonging to the hospital* will be immediately

THE HOSPITAL STEWARD'S MANUAL. 89

followed by that of those who, since last muster, *have ceased to belong to it.* These will be classed in the following order,—viz.: *Discharged, Transferred, Died, Deserted;* and the *utmost particularity* will be observed in the *remarks* concerning them. *Date* and *place* will, *in every case,* be given; and *No., date,* &c., of *orders,* or *description of authority,* be always carefully specified. Soldiers discharged *and re-enlisted,* or who have deserted *and been retaken,* since last muster, have their place in *both* of the above rolls.

7. The remark "*discharge and final statements given*" will be made opposite to the name of every discharged soldier to whom such papers *have actually been given.* But the blank spaces under the head of " Last Paid" are to be filled as usual.

8. In all cases of "*re-enlistment*" prior to the expiration of the term of service, the *discharge* on the old enlistment will be given at the time the soldier "re-enlists,"—from and on which day his pay on the *new* enlistment will commence.

9. Within *three days* after each regular muster, the mustering officer or commandant of the post will transmit to the Adjutant-General a copy of the *muster roll* of each company. Blanks will be supplied from the Adjutant-General's office, and will be *acknowledged* on the first muster roll forwarded after their receipt.

8*

90 THE HOSPITAL STEWARD'S MANUAL.

The roll has appended to it this recapitulation :—

RECAPITULATION.		Steward.	Ward-master.	Cooks.	Nurses.	Matrons.	Total.	
ABSENT. PRESENT.	{ For duty................							Total last muster.
	Sick........................							
	In arrest or confinement...							
	On detached service.........							
	With leave.................							
	Without leave..............							
	Sick........................							
	In arrest or confinement...							

STRENGTH—PRESENT AND ABSENT.

ALTERATIONS SINCE LAST MUSTER.	JOINED.	Recruits from depots........							No. of blank muster rolls on hand.
		Enlisted in hospital........							
		By re-enlistment............							
		By transfer, or app't.......							
		From desertion..............							
	DISCHARGED.	Resigned....................							
		Expiration of service.......							
		For disability..............							
		By sentence of G.C. Martial							
		By civil authority..........							
		By order....................							
		Transferred.................							
	DIED.	Killed in action............							
		Of wounds...................							
		From disease, &c............							
		Deserted....................							

The whole is certified to in the following form :—

I CERTIFY, ON HONOR, that this Muster Roll is made out in the manner required by the printed notes; that it exhibits the true state of the Hospital Department for the period herein mentioned; that the "Remarks" set opposite each name are accurate and just; and that the "Recapitulation" exhibits in every particular the true state of the hospital, as required by the Regulations and the Rules and Articles of War.

Surgeon in charge of Hospital.

STATION : _____

DATE : _____

I CERTIFY, ON HONOR, that I have carefully examined this Muster Roll; that I have mustered and minutely inspected the hospital attendants; and that the police and general condition of the Hospital Department is found to be as follows:

Inspector and Mustering Officer.

SECTION VI.—OF THE GUARD.

In camps and post hospitals the guard is furnished from the troops for whose benefit the hospital is established; it is under the orders of the officer of the day, and need not, therefore, be made the subject of remark in this place.

In detached general hospitals only, however, the guard, consisting of one or more non-commissioned officers, and a sufficient number of privates, according to the number of posts, is furnished to the hospital on the application of the surgeon to the commanding officer, with orders to report to the surgeon under whose command they remain.

The number of posts is determined by the surgeon. There should always be a sentinel posted at each entrance to the hospital, with orders to allow no patients or attendants to leave the building, except when furnished with a written pass, signed by the surgeon. Orders should also be given to admit no one, except patients or attendants returning from pass; new patients arriving with proper orders for admission; persons known to have business in the hospital; the medical officers and those wishing to see them; and visitors on the visiting days and hours only.

Besides these, sentinels may be placed on such other posts as in the opinion of the surgeon may be necessary.

The guard should live in the hospital, or in tents erected near it, as is most convenient in the opinion of the surgeon.

They are taken up on the hospital provision return, and obtain their meals at the general table for the convalescents and attendants.

SECTION VII.—OF THE GUARD-HOUSE.

In all general hospitals of any size, there should be a place set aside for the confinement of those guilty of drunkenness, disobedience to orders, or other military offences.

Where possible, this should be in a separate building, and is then called the guard-house; a sentinel should be posted before the door. Where this is not possible, a room should be employed for the purpose, and is known as the guard-room.

No patients or attendants should be confined except on order of the medical officers, or by the steward, who will immediately report the case to the surgeon in charge: all other attendants must report delinquents to the surgeon, or steward, for punishment, and not confine them themselves.

In these punishments the surgeon is, of course, guided by the same laws and regulations as apply in other cases to the punishment of the offences of enlisted men by commanding officers.

SECTION VIII.—RULES AND REGULATIONS FOR THE GOVERNMENT OF MILITARY HOSPITALS.

In every hospital, a code of rules and regulations should be drawn up by the surgeon in charge, printed upon large cards, and affixed to the walls in each ward, and in other conspicuous places. The following is an illustration of the form which may be employed. It should receive such modifications as local causes may make necessary to adapt it to any given hospital.

Rules and Regulations for the Government of the United States Army General Hospital at ———.

1. No patient will be allowed to leave the hospital without permission from the surgeon in charge. The same rule will hold with respect to nurses and other attendants.

2. No pass will be issued except between the hours of 10 A. M. and 12 M., except in urgent cases. The pass will be shown to the sentinel on post, and retained by the person receiving it until his return, when it will be given to the sentinel.

3. No smoking, swearing, or loud talking will be permitted in the wards and passages of this hospital; and spitting on the floor, or defacing the building in any way, is positively forbidden.

4. The beds will be made every morning by the attendants, or oftener, if necessary. Patients able to do so will, however, make their own beds.

5. No patient will occupy his bed without undressing.

6. Every patient, who is able, will wash his face and hands at least every morning, and

keep the rest of his body in a cleanly condition. Those who are unable to do this will have it done for them by the attendants. Every patient whose condition does not forbid it will take a bath on his admission into the hospital.

7. During the morning visit of the medical officer, every patient and nurse must be in the ward; nor will the former leave it before his visit. Patients who are able, will rise when the medical officer enters the ward, and remain standing at the sides of their beds until prescribed for or otherwise ordered.

8. No loud noises or improper language will be allowed in the wards at any time. All talking will cease at 8½ P.M., when all patients and nurses, except those of the latter on duty, will go to bed.

9. All lights in the hospital, except those in the offices and surgery, will be lowered at 9 P.M. All other lights will be extinguished at taps, unless otherwise directed by the attending medical officer.

10. No patients or nurses will be allowed to enter the office, surgery, or kitchen, unless on business connected with their duties. Lounging about the halls is also forbidden.

11. No persons will be allowed to enter the

hospital without special permission from the surgeon in charge, or the medical officer of the day.

12. No provisions or spirituous liquors of any kind shall be brought within the hospital without permission of the medical officer of the day. Nor will any relatives or friends of patients be allowed to give such articles to them, without permission from the medical officers of the ward.

13. Patients will give prompt obedience to the steward, ward-master, and nurses, in all lawful commands. Any infractions of discipline, disobedience of orders, drunkenness, or disorderly conduct, will be promptly punished.

CHAPTER II.

Police and General Supervision in Hospitals.

SECTION I.—CLEANLINESS OF THE HOSPITAL.

The hospital, hospital grounds, and all its appurtenances, must be maintained in a state of cleanliness as complete as possible.

Cleanliness of the floors is to be obtained by scrubbing or sweeping.

The whole hospital should be carefully and completely *swept* at least once daily, and as much oftener as dirt or litter accumulating in particular localities renders it necessary. The wards are swept by one of the attendants, the chief nurse being responsible for the proper performance of the duty; the kitchen, by one of its attendants, the chief cook being responsible; the dining-room, by one of the attendants assigned to duty there; and the halls, passages, stairs, offices, &c., by attendants specially assigned to the duty.

For the proper performance of this duty throughout the hospital, the steward must remember that *he* is responsible, and he must hold subordinates charged with its execution to a strict accountability.

Sweeping should be effectual, but should be executed in such a manner as not to fill the atmosphere with dust.

The broom should not be recklessly used, but should be carried steadily and gently over the floor, bearing the dust before it. Where there is much dust, the floor may be sprinkled before being swept, or the broom may be dipped lightly into water. The dirt should not be swept from wards or other apartments into the passages, but should be carried away in dust-pans.

Scrubbing is not so generally available as sweeping: the objection to it is that it leaves the floor damp for a considerable time afterwards. It is, however, to be resorted to whenever necessary to effect cleanliness. Sand may be used to advantage in scrubbing well-made floors. The reckless use of water is to be avoided. It soaks through the cracks of the floor into apartments below, if there are any, and leaves unnecessary dampness behind.

Where the condition of the floor is not very bad, the *use of a wet mop* may be substituted for scrubbing, requiring less time for its execution, and not leaving so much dampness.

Either scrubbing or mopping should, whenever possible, be done in clear, dry weather, (on good drying-days.)

Certain portions of the hospitals require special attention to preserve their cleanliness.

The *kitchen* should be swept out after each meal, or as much oftener as necessary.

The *dining-room*, after each meal.

The water-closets should be not only swept, but mopped or scrubbed, daily.

The walks around the hospitals should be swept daily. No garbage or filth should be allowed to collect in any place around the buildings.

Not merely the floors, but the walls, the ceilings, and the windows of the hospital require to be kept carefully clean.

The walls should be dusted from time to time, and kept free from dirt and cobwebs. Writing upon or otherwise disfiguring the walls or woodwork must be strictly prohibited. White-washing must be resorted to whenever necessary to maintain neatness. The whitewash should not merely be composed of lime and water, but should have salt or glue added to it, to make it less liable to rub or crack off.

Painted woodwork should be wiped, whenever soiled, with a damp cloth, and scrubbed when necessary.

The windows should be washed whenever their condition indicates the necessity. Once a week is, generally, often enough. Here, as with regard to scrubbing, a caution may be given against the reckless and excessive use of water.

SECTION II.—VENTILATION.

The steward is also responsible to the surgeon for the effective condition of the means of ventilation, whatever these may be.

In the best-constructed hospitals, ridge-ventilation, conjoined with ventilators flush with the floor, is the plan resorted to. The steward should notice, whenever he enters a ward, that the floor-ventilators are sufficiently open to secure a constant change of the air of the apartment. In rainy weather the ventilators on the windward side of the building should be so partially or completely closed as to prevent rain from beating in upon the floor of the apartment.

Where other means of ventilation are resorted to, attention is to be paid to their construction; and if the steward does not understand the principle upon which they act, he should apply to the surgeon for such explanations as will enable him intelligently to undertake their regulation.

In hotels, private houses, and other buildings temporarily used as hospitals, in which no means of ventilation except the windows, doors, and fireplaces exist, special care is necessary. In the summer-time the windows should be raised at the bottom and let down at the top. The doors should be kept open. The fireplaces and chimneys should be free from obstructions.

In the winter the windows should be let down at the top, but not so far as to render the ward too cold.

The cleanliness and ventilation of the wards should be such that a person entering them from the open air should not perceive the slightest close or unpleasant odor. Whenever the steward, in going his rounds, perceives such an odor, its cause should be investigated, and the necessary steps at once taken to remedy it.

A few statements may here be made to give the steward an idea of the amount of ventilation required to obtain the best results.

Each patient in hospital should have allotted to him from one thousand to fifteen hundred cubic feet of space. A thousand cubic feet will be secured by allowing to each bed a floor-surface six feet wide by twelve long, in an apartment in which the ceiling is thirteen and eight-ninths feet high.

Twelve hundred cubic feet will be secured by allowing each bed a floor-surface of seven feet by twelve in an apartment fourteen and two-sevenths feet high.

Thus, in a ward twenty-four feet wide and of either of the above heights, there may be two rows of beds, one on each side of the ward, the beds separated from each other by at least three or four feet. Where the ceilings are lower, a greater floor-surface should be allowed to each bed.

The number of beds in each ward is, therefore, of serious importance. It should be in every case determined by the surgeon, and, once having been established, should not be deviated from except by his express orders.

It is, however, of no avail to obtain for the

patient sufficient cubic space unless the ventilation is such as to obtain the requisite *change of air*. It has been calculated that each patient takes into his lungs, and throws out contaminated and unfit to be breathed again, from three to four hundred cubic feet per hour. If to this large element of contamination be added the deterioration of the atmosphere of the ward, resulting from the cutaneous exhalations of the sick, and the effluvia from suppurating wounds, offensive discharges, &c., it will be seen at a glance that the air of a hospital-ward must become rapidly unfit for use. The great object of ventilation is to produce such a steady and constant change of air as will cause the continual renewal of the contaminated ward-atmosphere by fresh supplies from without. It has been estimated that for this purpose each patient requires a supply of fresh air at the rate of at least double the cubic space above mentioned, or from two to three thousand cubic feet, per hour.

These conditions cannot be neglected or overlooked without inevitable injury to the sick, manifested in the type of disease, as well as by slowness of recovery and increase of mortality.

In certain cases the use of disinfectants will be needed in addition to careful cleanliness and ventilation,—especially in wards containing patients with malignant fevers or with suppurating wounds. In all such cases, however, the use of disinfectants should be ordered by the surgeon, and not resorted to by the steward or other nurses upon their own responsibility.

Hospital tents should be ventilated by ripping one or more seams near the ridge-pole of the tent, the rips to be about eighteen inches long: the gap may be propped open by a notched stick. Rain is prevented from entering by the tent fly.

This precaution should always be taken in hospital tents which are full of patients; but it is especially necessary when the tent is heated in the winter-time, either by a stove or the trenched fireplace described in the next section.

SECTION III.—THE WARMING OF THE HOSPITAL.

The steward is responsible, during the colder portion of the year, for the proper management of the means employed to warm the hospital. In order that this may be satisfactorily and efficiently done, a thermometer should hang in every ward. The proper temperature should be indicated by the surgeon. About 70° to 72° Fahrenheit is that usually ordered.

This temperature may be obtained in well-organized general hospitals by properly constructed furnaces, or by a steam heating-apparatus. In the great majority of the general hospitals at present organized in the United States, however, it is effected by stoves.

The more complicated and complete means of warming will, therefore, be passed by in the present work, with the remark that, if they be adopted in any general hospital, they should be so regulated as to keep the wards steadily at the required temperature, neither being, on the one hand, so managed as to have them at times unnecessarily warm, nor, on the other, so neglected as to allow them to cool more than at the most a very few degrees below the standard.

Stoves used for warming hospitals may be made for burning either wood or coal. The latter are preferable where coal can conveniently be obtained.

The chief nurse of each ward is responsible to the steward for the due maintenance of the fires and the temperature of the wards. Fuel is carried from the place in which it is stored, by one or more of the attendants, under the order of the chief nurse.

Care must be taken to keep the stoves neat and well blacked, to avoid dropping fragments of fuel upon the floor about the stoves, and to remove the ashes from time to time, as it becomes necessary, making always as little dust as possible.

To counteract the unnatural dryness of the atmosphere produced by the use of stoves, a vessel of water should be set on the top of each.

The stoves in the wards should on no account be used for cooking.

Hospital tents may also be warmed by stoves. It is perhaps preferable to warm them in the following manner:—

A trench is dug through the middle of the tent, about eighteen inches deep, and twelve to sixteen wide. This trench should extend about four feet beyond the tent at either extremity. The trench is covered over with pieces of sheet-iron, supported by iron cross-bars, the iron for this purpose to be obtained from the quartermaster on special requisition by the surgeon.

108 THE HOSPITAL STEWARD'S MANUAL.

A chimney is built of sods or mud at the highest extremity of the tent; a pit about two and a half feet deep and three long by two wide is sunk at the other for a fireplace. A wood fire being now built in this pit, the draft carries the flame and smoke along the trench beneath the hospital tent, which is thus not only warmed, but the ground on which it stands is thoroughly dried.

The fire will serve also to cook for the hospital.

Care must be taken not to overheat the tent, which is likely to happen when this method is used, unless ventilation at the top of the tent is resorted to, as described in the last section.

SECTION IV.—LIGHTING THE HOSPITAL.

Hospitals may be illuminated by candles, by lamps, or by gas.

Gas is beyond question the most satisfactory method of illumination. As usually employed, it is also the most expensive. This is to a great extent the result of unnecessary extravagance; and the gas-lights should therefore be carefully supervised by the stewards. No more gas-jets should be illuminated than are absolutely necessary for the business of the house, and these should have no more gas turned on than is necessary. At nine o'clock all the burners should be extinguished except a single one in each ward, which should be so regulated as to give but a feeble flame, like that of a candle, and a few in the passages and on the staircases, to enable attendants on duty to go about the buildings. The gas-bill is paid out of the hospital fund.

Lamps suspended from the ceiling, or fixed upon the wall at convenient places, are, next to gas, the most desirable means of illumination. Camphene or burning-fluid lamps should be avoided as dangerous, and whale-oil, lard-oil, or coal-oil lamps preferred. Coal oil has recently been extensively used for illuminating purposes, and furnishes perhaps the cheapest and most satisfactory illuminating fluid. The oil is paid for out of the hospital fund.

Where lamps are used, they should be cleaned, trimmed, and filled daily. This may be done by the attendants in the ward; but in a hospital of any size it is much better to detail one or more attendants, whose special duty it shall be to collect daily all the lamps of the hospital, clean, trim, and fill them, and to return them to their places, for the due execution of which duties they are responsible to the steward.

Where neither gas nor lamps can conveniently be obtained, it becomes necessary to use candles. Candles for this purpose are drawn from the commissary on the hospital provision return. Adamantine candles are to be preferred for general use; but a small stock of sperm candles should be kept on hand for special purposes, as, for instance, the occasion of any surgical operations necessarily performed at night.

SECTION V.—THE LATRINES.

The latrines require careful attention, and their supervision is an important part of the duties of the hospital steward.

In every general hospital there should be well-constructed water-closets attached to each ward. These should be kept scrupulously dry and clean, the urinals and seats free from filth, and the apparatus at all times in good working order. Any defects or breakage should be at once reported to the surgeon. The water-closet should at all times be free from any offensive smell.

It will be found advisable in large institutions to keep an attendant constantly on guard before the entrance of each water-closet, whose duty it shall be to inspect its condition after every patient, in order that all neglects of propriety or cleanliness may be fixed at once upon the guilty party.

In temporary hospitals it is not always possible to secure such costly accommodations: a very good substitute may then be made, as follows: a small frame building is constructed outside of the hospital building; in this is placed a trough twelve to twenty feet long, lined with zinc and covered with a movable lid, in which from four to ten oval holes are cut.

One end of the trough should be higher than the other. At the higher end is a faucet to let in water; at the lower, a pipe, six to eight inches in diameter, which should run obliquely to a deep sink dug down to the gravel, and carefully covered. Lime or some other disinfectant should be thrown into this sink at least once a week, and when it is filled to within six feet of the surface it should be abandoned, filled in with earth, mixed with lime, and a new sink constructed. Such sinks should never be dug in the neighborhood of wells.

In camp hospitals even this simple arrangement is not practicable, and ordinary camp sinks must be used. These should be dug at some distance from the hospital tents. They should be each about ten feet long, two feet wide, and six deep. A crotched stick is driven into the ground at each end, and a pole laid across to serve as a seat. Every day a little earth is thrown in to cover the ordure of the day previous, and when filled to within two feet of the surface the sink should be abandoned, filled up with lime and earth, and a new sink constructed.

Where possible, a small shed should be erected over each sink, to protect patients during inclement weather. Where lumber cannot be obtained for this purpose, a screen of boughs should be erected, to protect the spot from observation.

SECTION VI.—OF THE BATHS AND LAVATORIES.

Wherever possible, general hospitals, even when only intended for temporary use, should be furnished with a bath-room; and in permanent institutions a bath-room should be attached to each ward. It should be supplied, wherever possible, with both hot and cold water. Cast-iron tubs answer an excellent purpose, and are readily kept in order, particularly if from time to time they receive a coat of paint.

The bath-room must be kept cleanly and free from all unnecessary slops, the bath-tubs neat and free from dirt of any kind. Patients should not be allowed to use the bath indiscriminately; the surgeon should indicate those who may use the ordinary cold bath, those who need the tepid bath, and those who should have the hot bath, and the frequency with which baths may be permitted.

For the great majority of patients, especially in cold weather, the bath should be tepid, the temperature being about 80° Fahrenheit. Where a warm bath is given, the greatest care should be taken to avoid unnecessary exposure of the patient to cold on leaving the bath. The bath-room should, if possible, be well warmed, the doors and windows closed to avoid drafts. When the patient leaves the bath, he should be wrapped at once in a warm blanket and put to bed. Water should not be allowed to stand in the bath-tubs after it has been used for a bath. It should be immediately emptied and the tub rinsed out, to prevent the sediment deposited from adhering to the bottom of the tub and rendering it permanently unclean.

The Lavatories are intended for convalescent patients and attendants to wash their hands and faces on rising in the morning, or at other times, when necessary to preserve cleanliness.

They should be in a separate apartment from the bath-room, whenever practicable. Where the hospital is not fitted up with a complete lavatory, specially designed for the purpose, a room should be prepared, with a long table or shelf, on which tin basins, with soap, towels, &c., may be placed for this purpose. Convalescents able to go to the dining-room for meals should be obliged to wash their hands and faces, and comb their hair, daily, before going to breakfast.

The same cleanliness so necessary everywhere in a hospital should be manifest in the lavatory. After the morning washing, the basins should be rinsed and dried, the shelf cleaned, the soap put into a vessel or vessels designed for its reception, and the shelf and floor carefully dried.

Patients unable to leave their beds should have their hands and faces washed daily by the nurses. General sponging of the surface and washing of the feet should be practised often enough to maintain cleanliness.

SECTION VII.—THE WARDS OF THE HOSPITAL, THEIR ARRANGEMENT AND ADMINISTRATION.

Hospital wards are of various sizes, and may accommodate from a very few to a great number of patients. From twenty to fifty is probably the most convenient number. The number of patients in any given ward is to be determined by the surgeon; and it is the duty of the steward to place in the ward the number of beds thus directed. The surgeon will base his allotment of beds upon an actual measurement of the apartment, allowing from one thousand to fifteen hundred cubic feet of space per bed wherever practicable.

The bedsteads, which are usually of iron in United States military hospitals, should not in any case be less than three feet apart, even when the height of the apartment gives the necessary cubic space if they are closer together.

The bed-furniture consists of a mattress or bedsack, sheets, blankets, a coverlet, pillow, and pillow-case.

The best mattresses are undoubtedly those stuffed with hair. They are the most comfortable, the most durable, and are less liable to become impregnated with unhealthy exhalations proceeding from the patients, and thus to give rise to disease in those subsequently occupying them, than any others. Their great comparative expense, however, prevents their adoption in such extensive establishments as those created by the existing war; and they are not, therefore, generally met with.

Where, however, they have been furnished, special care should be used for their preservation, oiled silk or oil-cloth or gutta-percha cloth being introduced between the sheet and the mattress in all cases in which the discharge from wounds, or the probability of hemorrhage, or any other cause, renders them liable to be soiled.

The mattress usually furnished by the medical purveyor consists of a ticking stuffed with corn-shucks either alone or mixed with straw. This is much less durable than the hair mattress. It is also much less expensive, and answers usually a very good purpose.

When it is soiled, or after it has been used by a patient laboring under typhoid or typhus fever, it should not be burned, as is frequently done, but, the contents having been emptied and destroyed, the tick, if its condition is good, should be retained, washed and boiled, and subsequently used as a bedsack.

Bedsacks are probably quite as useful as the mattresses last described. They are certainly less expensive. They should be filled with clean straw, carefully introduced, so as to break up the stems as little as possible. The great advantage of bedsacks over any kind of mattresses is that they may be frequently emptied, the sack washed and its contents renewed. This, on the other hand, implies continual attention and considerable labor; and there can be no doubt that neglected bedsacks form as uncomfortable and unwholesome a couch as could possibly be furnished a sick man.

Where bedsacks are used, the straw should be renewed at least once a month for convalescents, attendants, and ordinary cases, and as much oftener for fever-cases, suppurating wounds, &c., as the nature of the case may require.

When the bedsack is emptied, it should never be filled again until it is washed and boiled.

"In barracks, twelve pounds of straw for bedding will be allowed to each man, servant, and company woman.

"The allowance and change of straw for the sick is regulated by the surgeon."*

Straw for this purpose is obtained from the quartermaster on a requisition signed by the surgeon.

Two sheets are allowed to each bed. For convalescents and attendants it will be sufficient if the lower sheet is removed each week and is replaced by the upper, which is to be replaced by a clean one. But for fever-cases, or where there are offensive discharges, the sheets should be changed as often as they are soiled or as the change is directed by the surgeon.

Each bed should be furnished with one

---

* Revised Reg., Art. XLII. ¿¿ 1126–1127

blanket in summer-time and two in winter, or with such additional ones as may be directed by the surgeon in special cases. The blankets should be changed and washed as often as they become soiled.

Each bed is furnished with a coverlet, which is usually of a woven white material. It should be changed whenever it becomes soiled.

To keep the white coverlet clean, patients should never be allowed to lie down on the bed with their clothes on.

One pillow is allowed to each bed, except in special cases, where additional ones are ordered by the attending surgeon. The pillow-case should be changed once a week, or as often as it is soiled.

The beds of all patients who are able to go to their meals in the mess-halls should be made up by themselves immediately after reveille. Those of patients unable to leave their beds should be made up from time to time, as the nature of the case may permit.

Each bed should have attached to it or suspended above it a ticket, on which is recorded the name, rank, regiment and company, disease, and date of admission of the patient, and on the reverse of which is a list of his personal effects. For the form of this ticket, see Part II. chap. iii. sect. 1.

Mosquito-nets should, so far as practicable, be furnished to every bed in those seasons and localities in which they are desirable. They should be kept carefully clean and in good repair.

The ward should also be furnished with a number of *small tables* or *stands*, upon which may be placed the medicines, &c. of the patients. One to every two beds is usually a sufficient number. Each serves, therefore, for two patients. These tables should be kept scrupulously clean, and nothing should be allowed upon them except such articles as are actually in use.

Chairs to the number of one to every bed, or at least one to every two beds, are generally supplied. These and the tables should have definite places assigned them, out of which they should never be found except when actually in use.

The spittoons, chamber-pots, and chamber-chairs should likewise be the subject of careful supervision. Spittoons should be emptied and washed out thoroughly every day; chamber-pots, bed-pans, urinals, and the receptacle of chamber-chairs, *every time* they are used.

In hospitals in which water-closets are not attached to each ward, every ward should have a small room partitioned off, into which patients may go to use the chamber chairs or pots, whenever practicable, in order that the odor which accompanies the evacuations may not be diffused throughout the ward.

The FLOOR of the ward should be constantly kept clean and neat, no litter or dirt being for a moment allowed upon it; nor should patients' clothes be suffered beneath the beds.

Each ward has allowed to it a certain number of attendants, which varies with the number of patients, one to every ten patients being the allowance of army regulations.*

The duties of these attendants are detailed in Part I. chap. iii. sect. 4.

SECTION VIII.—THE OFFICE OF THE HOSPITAL.

An apartment convenient to the entrance of the hospital is set aside as the office, in which the records and papers of the institution are kept, and where general business-matters

---

* Revised Reg., Art. XLIX. ¿ 1258.

connected with the establishment are transacted.

The regulations direct that "the senior medical officer of each hospital, post, regiment, or detachment will keep the following records, and deliver them to his successor. A register of patients; a prescription book; a diet book; a case book; a meteorological register; copies of his requisitions, annual returns, and quarterly reports of sick and wounded; and an order and letter book, in which will be transcribed all orders and letters relating to his duties.

"He will make up the muster and pay rolls of the medical cadets, hospital steward, female nurses, and matrons, and of all soldiers in hospital, sick or on duty, detached from their companies, on the forms furnished from the Adjutant-General's office, and according to the directions expressed on them. He will make the rolls of the cooks and nurses for extra-duty pay, which will be paid by the paymaster, in the absence of a medical disbursing officer, as in other cases of expenditures for the medical department."*

---

* Revised Reg., Art. XLIV. §§ 1254-1256.

Practically, a large part of these records are kept either by one of the stewards, or by one or more attendants selected by the surgeon for the purpose, and who are, in fact, the *clerks* of the hospital,—an office which is not formally recognized by law or regulations.

A few remarks may be made on each of these heads.

The Register of Patients.

This record should be kept in a book properly ruled for the purpose in accordance with the form prescribed by regulations. Such books can, under ordinary circumstances, be obtained from the medical purveyor on requisition by the surgeon. The form is as follows:—

Register.	Names.	Rank.	Regiment or corps.	Company.	Complaint.	Admitted.	Returned to duty.	Deserted.	Discharged from service.	Sent to general hospital.	On furlough.	Died.	Ward.	Bed.	Remarks.

N.B.—Both Christian and surname will be registered.

This register should be carefully kept. The names of patients should be entered immediately on their admission, with their rank, regiment, and company, and the number of the ward and bed. The diagnosis should not be entered until subsequently, and never by the steward or clerk upon his own responsibility, but only on instructions received from the surgeons.

The steward should look over the register once, weekly, and, whenever omissions exist in the diagnosis, should present the book to the surgeons in charge of the several wards, for the necessary entries.

The subsequent columns, of course, can only be filled up on the termination of the case.

The register thus kept furnishes the data from which the monthly and quarterly reports of sick and wounded are made out.

In large general hospitals some additional means should, however, be resorted to, to enable friends or others looking for individual patients to find them without difficulty.

To effect this purpose, an alphabetical index to the register must be kept, in which will be entered the name, regiment, and company of each patient, with the page of the register on which his name is to be found.

As the *Prescription* and *Diet Book*, as well as the *Case Book*, are kept by the surgeon in person, it is not necessary to discuss them in this work.

The Meteorological Register.—Keeping this register is a duty which, although supposed to be performed by the surgeon, is frequently executed by the hospital steward under his supervision. Books properly ruled for this purpose are obtained on the surgeon's requisition upon the medical purveyor. Where the meteorological record is kept by the steward, the surgeon will always make full explanations as to the manner in which this duty is performed, and will supervise his procedures from time to time, to ascertain their correctness. The subject need not, therefore, be entered into in detail.

The copies of *requisitions, annual returns,* and *quarterly reports of sick and wounded* are to be kept carefully on file.

The Order and Letter Book is to retain copies, not merely of all letters and reports received, but of all written by the surgeon in charge, on official business.

Besides these records prescribed in regulations, it will be found convenient to keep among the hospital books three separate lists of *discharges, furloughs, and deaths.* In a large hospital each of these subjects should have a special book devoted to it.*

The Muster and Pay Rolls of the cadets, hospital stewards, female nurses, matrons, and of soldiers in hospital, sick or on duty, are made out every two months by one of the clerks or hospital stewards. When it is completed, it is signed by the surgeon in charge, after having carefully inspected it, and *mustered* the patients and attendants to satisfy himself that the rolls are perfectly correct.

For the forms of these several rolls, see Part I.

Of Passes.—Patients or attendants desiring to leave the hospital for any purpose, must obtain a written pass from the surgeon on duty as officer of the day, or from the surgeon in charge, under such rules and regulations as may be established for each hospital.

SECTION IX.—THE KNAPSACK-ROOM.

The knapsack-room is a place set apart for the safe keeping, not only of the knapsacks,

---

* See Part II. chap. iii.

but of the overcoats, blankets, and other property of the patients, and of their arms and accoutrements when they are brought with them to the hospital.

It should be a secure apartment, of sufficient size, shelved on all sides and furnished with an arms-rack for the arms.

Certain shelves should be set aside for each ward. On these the knapsacks should be neatly arranged. Each should be carefully and regularly packed, the articles having been first well cleaned or washed, if necessary. A label should be attached, having written legibly upon it the name of the owner, with his regiment and company. Great-coats and blankets should be neatly folded and strapped upon the knapsack.

Arms should be placed in order upon the arms-rack, and a similar label attached to each musket, sabre, belt, &c.

Patients on going to hospital should, however, when possible, leave their arms and accoutrements with their companies, and on no account take ammunition into the hospital.*

The care of the knapsack-room, the reception

---

* Revised Regulations, Art. XLIV. § 1251.

of the articles from the patient, and their due delivery to him when he leaves the hospital, are duties for the proper performance of which the *ward-master* to whom they are intrusted is responsible to the steward. The knapsack-room should be opened from time to time, swept, dusted, and well aired.

SECTION X.—THE LAUNDRY.

The washing of hospitals is a subject of very considerable importance, and requires careful supervision. Whenever practicable, it should be done in the hospital, in a room set aside for that purpose and designated as the laundry. The washing should never be given out when it can be avoided. Want of punctuality and of responsibility on the part of the laundresses are the objections.

The laundresses are appointed by the surgeon in charge of a general hospital. Soldiers' wives should have the preference. They receive for their services $6 per month, with one ration per day.

Laundresses are usually employed in general hospitals in the proportion of one to every twenty beds. In the practical duties of their service the best results will be attained if the matron in charge of the linen-room issues a certain number of pieces to each as her day's task, holding her responsible for their proper condition when returned.

Washing for a great hospital is probably best and most economically effected by steam, as is practised in various British military and naval establishments.

At the present time, however, there are few establishments in the United States which possess the necessary apparatus for this purpose, and the washing has to be effected in a much simpler manner.

Large-sized caldrons, holding about fifty gallons, with a small furnace attached, are issued by the medical purveyors or the quartermaster, for the purpose of boiling those articles which require this treatment. The washing is effected in troughs made for the purpose, or in ordinary wash-tubs, as the case may be. Washing-machines of various sorts are used in some of the hospitals. The processes will necessarily vary so much in accordance with the apparatus supplied to the hospital, that no general rules can be laid down in this place. It need only be said that the clothes are to be washed clean, without exposing them to unnecessary violence, carefully dried, and neatly ironed.

The furniture of the laundry should consist, according to the size of the hospital, of one or more clothes-boilers (fifty-gallon caldrons), with furnace attached, one or more stoves for heating smoothing-irons, for which a special stove is issued by the medical purveyor, and of a sufficient number of wash-tubs, which may be either fixed troughs of wood lined with tin or zinc, with the faucets for hot and cold water supply immediately over them, or, where this is not attainable, may be simply round tubs of the ordinary pattern, set upon benches of convenient size.

There will be needed, besides, wash-boards, ironing-boards, ironing-tables, and smoothing-irons.

The laundry should be in charge of one of the laundresses, designated for the purpose. She should be responsible for its order and neatness, should give general superintendence to the work, and be authorized to issue the necessary directions to insure its efficient execution.

SECTION XI.—THE LINEN-ROOM.

The room in which the clean bedclothes, under-clothes, &c. are stored when not in use, is generally called the linen-room; and this designation may be conveniently retained, although a large majority of the articles stored away are made of muslin or other materials, and not of linen.

The linen-room should be shelved round conveniently for the reception of the articles stored, and should be furnished with a lock and key for security. It should be placed in charge of a female nurse, with one or more assistants, according to the size of the institution.

On taking charge of the linen-room, the nurse should be furnished with a list of the articles intrusted to her care, which she should verify by personal inspection. Subsequently, she should keep a memorandum-book, in which the chief nurse of each ward should be charged with all articles issued to him for his ward, and credited by all soiled articles received from him at the soiled-clothes closet, which should also be under her charge, so that she shall superintend on the one hand the

THE HOSPITAL STEWARD'S MANUAL. 133

issue of clean articles to the ward, and their return soiled, and on the other the issue of soiled articles to the laundresses, and their return clean.

But in neither case should she allow articles to go out of her hand without a memorandum made, setting forth the number of each article issued, and the person responsible.

The chief articles which will thus pass through her hands are—

Sheets, coverlets, blankets, bed-sacks, pillow-cases, towels, mosquito-nets, and hospital suits, consisting of shirts, drawers, and socks. All these articles should be marked U. S. Hosp. Dept., with indelible ink.

Besides these articles of hospital property, it is usual for the soiled clothes of patients to be washed in the laundry.

The female nurse in charge of the linen-room, with her assistants, should also be required to see that the articles are in a proper state of repair, and, if not, to mend them carefully before issuing.

CHAPTER III.

Admissions, Discharges, Deaths, &c.

SECTION I.—ADMISSION OF PATIENTS.

PATIENTS are to be received into hospitals only when sent there by competent authority, except in extreme cases, in the discretion of the surgeon.

Each patient should be accompanied by the written order for his admission, and by his descriptive list.

The patients are received either by the steward, or by a medical officer detailed for that duty (the medical officer of the day).

If the patient is able to walk, he is taken into the office, and his name, rank, regiment, or corps, and the date of admission, entered in the hospital register. His effects are then turned over to the ward-master (and his money or any valuables given to the surgeon for safe keeping); after which he is taken to the bath-room, thoroughly cleansed, his head and clothes examined for vermin, and measures taken for their destruction if any are observed.

He is then taken to the ward and bed assigned to him.

A ticket has meantime been made out for him in the office, which contains on its face his name, rank, regiment or corps, company, and date of admission, with a blank space, on which the surgeon may enter the diagnosis.

On the reverse is a list of his effects. A convenient form for these tickets is as follows:—

(*Face of the Ticket.*)

NUMBER OF BED:

....

NAME:

....

COMPANY:

....

REGIMENT:

....

DISEASE OR INJURY.

....

DATE OF ADMISSION.

....

DATE OF DISCHARGE.

....

WHERE SENT, AND BY WHAT AUTHORITY.

....

(*Reverse.*)

CLOTHING, &c.

	No.		No.
Knapsacks...		Drawers, prs..	
Great Coat...		Bootees, prs..	
Blanket....		Boots, prs...	
Uniform Coat.		Stockings, prs.	
Undress Coat.		Money....	
Trousers...			
Shirts.....			

This ticket, properly filled up, is placed at the head of the patient's bed, where it is to remain so long as he remains in hospital. It may simply be fastened to the wall with a tack; but it is more convenient to have a little tin plate, with the edges on three sides turned over, so as to form a frame, into which the ticket may be slipped. The frame to be fastened to the head-piece of the bed, or hung upon the wall above it.

Tickets printed in blank for this purpose, as well as the frames, may be purchased by the surgeon out of the hospital fund, when not supplied by the purveyor.

When the patient is unable to walk, the steps to be taken are essentially the same, modified only in accordance with the necessity of the case. He is to be taken carefully from the ambulance in which he was brought to the hospital, by gently drawing out the litter on which he lies, and laying it upon the ground. He is then transferred to a hand-stretcher and carried into the hospital. If his condition is such that it is not advisable to bathe him,—of which, whenever practicable, a medical officer should be the judge,—he should be carried at once to the ward and bed assigned him, undressed, and put into the bed, taking such measures to secure cleanliness, by washing the head, hands, and feet, changing the underclothes, &c., as may be possible under the circumstances. If the patient is severely wounded, and especially if bones are fractured, the greatest care should be employed in handling him, and in carrying the stretcher. The stretcher should be carried by two strong attendants, who should be directed to step off in such a manner that when the foremost puts his right foot forward the hindmost shall put forward his left: by so doing, much unnecessary jolting and tilting of the stretcher will be avoided.

If stairs are to be ascended, the foremost bearer should lower his end of the stretcher, while the hindmost elevates his in such a manner as to keep the patient as nearly on a level as possible. The reverse is to be done if stairs are to be descended.

The patient received into hospital should, if thereby separated from his company so as not to be mustered with it for pay, be accompanied with his descriptive list and account of pay and clothing. If this does not come with him, the steward should at once bring the fact to the notice of the surgeon, who will address a note on the subject to the company commander, whose duty it is to furnish it.

The descriptive lists and accounts of pay and clothing of soldiers received into hospital are to be carefully filed away in the office of the hospital, in order that the surgeon, as required by regulations, may enter thereon "all payments, stoppages, and issues of clothing to him in hospital."*

The form of the descriptive list and account of pay and clothing is the same for enlisted men as for hospital stewards.†

SECTION II.—RETURN TO DUTY—TRANSFER TO THEIR HOSPITALS—FURLOUGHS AND DISCHARGES.

The patient thus received into hospital may either recover, remain incurable, or at least permanently disabled, or may die.

If he recovers, he will be sent back immediately to his company by the surgeon, unless otherwise directed by proper authority. When sent back to his company, the date is entered in the register under the head "*returned to duty.*"

---

* Revised Reg., Art. XLIV. § 1250.
† See Part I. Chap. I. § 3.

Sometimes, on account of the crowded or unhealthy state of the hospital, he is transferred to another hospital. This is usually done by order of the medical director of the military district, on application of the surgeon in charge, or otherwise. In this case, the date should be entered in the register under the head "*sent to general hospital*," and a memorandum should be made in the column of remarks of the hospital to which he is sent and the authority by which the transfer was made.

When it is deemed desirable in tedious cases, or during convalescence, the patient may be allowed to leave the hospital *on furlough*. The furlough is obtained on application made to the commanding officer by the surgeon, accompanied by a certificate of the nature of the complaint in consequence of which the application is made, and setting forth the time which, in the surgeon's opinion, must elapse before he will be fit for duty. When a patient leaves the hospital on furlough, the date should be entered in the hospital register in the column "*on furlough*." The time for which the furlough is granted should be entered in the column of remarks.

If the patient is believed by the surgeon to be suffering from such a complaint or disability as to justify his discharge from service, he makes out a "certificate of disability for discharge," in accordance with the prescribed form, Med. Regulations, Form 13, and forwards it to the proper authority, as directed in army regulations.*

When the patient is discharged from service, the date will be entered in the register in the column "*discharged from service,*" and the reasons set forth in the certificate of disability are to be entered in the column of remarks.

When the patient leaves the hospital, "the medical officer shall certify and remit his descriptive list, showing the state of his accounts. If he is discharged from service in hospital, the surgeon shall make out his final statement for pay and clothing."†

Patients may also occasionally desert from hospital. Every patient who remains absent from hospital, without leave, for more than three days, should be regarded as a deserter. A separate column in the register of patients,

---

* Revised Reg., Art. XIX.
† Revised Reg., Art. XLIV. § 1250.

marked "*deserted*," is prepared for the entry of the date of desertion.

SECTION III.—OF DEATHS.

When a patient dies in hospital, the corpse should not be allowed to remain in the ward, but be at once removed to some convenient place assigned for its reception.

Almost all general hospitals have an apartment or separate building (the dead-house) set aside for this purpose.

The greatest decency and decorum should characterize these measures, and every respect should be paid by the attendants to the corpse.

If desired, the body may be delivered to the friends of the deceased by the surgeon. If not, he at once applies to the quartermaster for means of burial.

When a patient dies in hospital, the surgeon is directed, by regulations, to take charge of his effects in trust for his legal representatives, and to "make the reports required in the general regulations concerning soldiers who die absent from their companies."*

---

* Revised Regulations, Art. XLIV. ₴ 1250. See also Art. XVII. ₴ 152.

The date of death is to be entered on the hospital register, in the column marked *died*.

The following regulations have been issued by the War Department on the subject:—

Regulations for Military Burials and the Registration of Deceased Soldiers and their Graves.

The friends of deceased soldiers desire that accurate and permanent registration be made of date, place of burial, transfers of corpse, and official orders respecting interment, to enable them to find the grave, and such records as are important for purposes of identification.

To attain these ends—

First. The hospital in which the soldier dies must preserve a sufficient and proper record.

Second. The Adjutant-General's office should receive a perfect duplicate of the same, as the records of that office would be more permanent than those of the hospitals or the cemeteries.

Third. The sextons, whether of churches or of military or other public cemeteries, should have permanent records, which shall always be accessible to the friends of the deceased.

The records of each of these officers should be kept alphabetically indexed for reference.

Each grave should have its number, in the

THE HOSPITAL STEWARD'S MANUAL. 145

order of interments, distinctly indicated upon a post or plank of cedar or some other enduring wood. The name of deceased, the date of death, and his company or regimental corps initials, should, if possible, be engraved upon the said post or plank. This should be effected with an iron letter-brand or stamp. These posts or head-boards, and the lettering of the name, &c., will be provided by the quartermaster of the department or military post where the hospital is located or where the death occurs.

THE DUTY OF MILITARY SURGEONS.

In accordance with the accompanying order of the Secretary of War, it becomes the duty of the senior surgeon for the hospital or the military company in which a soldier dies, *immediately* after the death, to cause the copies of Record—1, 2, and 3—to be accurately made out, and to forward copy No. 3 to the quartermaster, or, in the absence of a quartermaster, to the commanding officer of the division or company in which the death has occurred.

Copy No. 2 shall be forwarded without delay to the Adjutant-General at Washington, by the surgeon, or by such other officer as the commander may designate. Generally, except in the District of Columbia, it will be the surgeon's duty to forward copy No. 2 to the local adjutant or commanding officer, who, after noting the contents, will place his signature upon the face of the surgeon's notification attached, and immediately forward it to the Adjutant-General.

Whenever a military hospital is finally broken up or vacated, the hospital records should all be transmitted to the Surgeon-General's office at Washington, and they must ever be open to the inspection of the friends of the deceased.

THE DUTY OF SEXTONS.

The sexton must be directed to preserve the records and the orders sent to him by the quartermaster. He must also be required to attend to the planting of the head-board or post furnished by the quartermaster for the grave of the deceased.

In all cemeteries in which deceased soldiers are interred, the burials should, if practicable, be made in regular series, occupying a separate plat of ground; but if otherwise and promiscuously interred, the numbers and description of the locality of the grave should be carefully recorded by the sexton.

The sexton should be required to notify the physician of the hospital of the number and locality of the grave before he takes the corpse.

In the case of a military burial at an encampment or upon a march, without the aid of a sexton, it shall be the duty of the commanding officer of the military corps to which the deceased belonged to cause his remains to be properly interred, and to provide suitable means for marking the grave and erecting a head-board with the proper inscription or stamped record. And, in the absence of a sexton, it shall be the duty of the adjutant or the commander of the said military corps to preserve the sexton's copy of record; and it will also be the duty of the surgeon to said corps to preserve the hospital copy of said record with the same care, and subject to the same conditions, as similar records in general or post hospitals.

In accordance with the foregoing regulations, the following forms are furnished :—

Hospital Record, subject to the order of the Surgeon-General of the United States Army.

No. 1.

RECORD OF DEATH AND INTERMENT.

Name and number of person interred	
Number and locality of the grave	
Hospital number of the deceased	
Regiment, rank, and company	
Residence before enlistment	
Conjugal condition (and if married, the residence of the widow)	
Cause of death	
Age of the deceased	
Nativity	
References and remarks	
Date of death and burial	186 .

Duplicates sent to the Adjutant-General of the United States Army, and to the Sexton of the .... Cemetery.

Memoranda:

THE HOSPITAL STEWARD'S MANUAL.   149

Copy of Record for the Adjutant-General, U. S. A.
No. 2.
RECORD OF DEATH AND INTERMENT.

Name and number of person interred	....
Number and locality of the grave......	....
Hospital number of the deceased......	....
Regiment, rank, and company.........	....
Residence before enlistment............	....
Conjugal condition (and if married, the residence of the widow)....... }	....
Cause of death................................ }	....
Age of the deceased.......................	....
Nativity..	....
References and remarks............... }	....
Date of death and burial................	.... 186 .

[A duplicate of this Record has been forwarded to the Sexton, and another remains at this Hospital.]

To ....
SIR:
It becomes my duty to inform you that the person above described died at this hospital as herein stated; and that it is desired his remains should be interred with the usual military honors.
                Respectfully,
                        ....,
                      Surgeon U. S. Army.
MILITARY HOSPITAL, ...

This copy of Record is to be transmitted to the Adjutant-General at Washington immediately after the place of burial and the number of the grave have been ascertained and registered. The above notification is to remain attached.

150 THE HOSPITAL STEWARD'S MANUAL.

Quartermaster's Notification of Death.

To ....

SIR:

I have the honor to inform you that ....
.............., a .... of Company ...., Regiment ...., died at this Hospital ...., and I would request you to make the necessary preparation for the interment of his remains as soon as practicable. The hour for the funeral is appointed at ....

..............................,
Surgeon U. S. Army.

..............................,
.............., 186 .

THE HOSPITAL STEWARD'S MANUAL.

The Sexton's Record and the Order for Burial.

No. 3.

RECORD OF DEATH AND INTERMENT.

Name and number of person interred	....
Number and locality of the grave......	....
Hospital number of the deceased......	....
Regiment, rank, and company..........	....
Residence before enlistment............	....
Conjugal condition, (and if married, the residence of the widow)....... }	....
Cause of death......................... }	....
Age of the deceased.....................	....
Nativity................................	....
Remarks and references............... }	....
Date of death and burial................	.... 186 .

To

The Sexton of ....

You will receive, and immediately inter, the remains of the person above described, and preserve this record, and also attend to the setting of the head-board at the grave, as provided by the Government and ordered by the Secretary of War.

....

Quartermaster.

[Burial from the ....]

This order for the burial is to remain attached to the Sexton's copy of Record as part of the record.

PART III.

FOOD FOR THE HOSPITAL AND ITS PREPARATION.—THE KITCHEN AND ITS MANAGEMENT.

CHAPTER I.

Provision Returns—Hospital Stores—Purchases for the Hospital—The Hospital Fund and its Management.

SECTION I.—PRELIMINARY.

THE financial principle upon which the hospitals of the United States armies are managed is, that sick soldiers in hospital ought not to cost more to the government than soldiers in the field; and, practically, it is found that the fund created by savings upon the full ration is amply sufficient, if properly managed, to suffice for the purchase of all those little comforts and delicacies which are necessaries for the sick.

The mode of procedure upon this subject directed in the Revised Regulations is as follows:—

The hospital is credited on the books of the commissary from which it draws its rations by the whole number of complete rations due throughout the month at the contract or cost price. It draws from the commissary only so much of each article issued by him as is actually required for the use of the sick and the attendants: this is charged against the hospital at the contract or cost price. The balance left, after deducting the total cost of provisions actually issued to the hospital from the total cost of the rations to which it is entitled, constitutes the "hospital fund," and this or any portion of it may be expended under the direction of the medical officer for any articles necessary either for the diet or for the comfort of the sick which are not authorized to be otherwise furnished.

As the economical management of the rations and the consequent creation of a hospital fund depends to a great extent upon the steward, an exposé of the details of the system is here introduced, which, it is believed, will be found sufficiently complete.

SECTION II.—OF THE RATION.

The ration authorized by army regulations is composed of the following articles and quantities:—

THE RATION.

"The ration is three-fourths of a pound of pork or bacon, or one and a fourth pound of fresh or salt beef; twenty-two ounces of bread or flour, or one pound of hard bread, or one and a fourth pound of corn meal; and at the rate, to every one hundred rations, of eight quarts of beans or peas *and* ten pounds of rice or hominy; ten pounds of green coffee, or eight pounds of roasted and ground coffee, or one and a half pound of tea; fifteen pounds of sugar; four quarts of vinegar; one pound of sperm candles, or one and a fourth pound of adamantine candles, or one and a half pound of tallow candles; four pounds of soap, and two quarts of salt. In addition to the foregoing, there is allowed twice per week one gallon of molasses per one hundred rations, and thrice per week, if practicable, an issue of potatoes, at the rate of one pound per man. When beans, peas, rice, hominy, or potatoes cannot be issued in the proportions given above, an equivalent in value shall be issued in some other proper food. Desiccated potatoes, or desiccated mixed vegetables, at the rate, per one hundred rations, of one hundred and fifty ounces of the former, or one hundred ounces of the latter, may be substituted for beans, peas, rice, hominy, or fresh potatoes, when these articles cannot be issued; or, upon the requisition of the proper officer and when the supply on hand will admit of it, they may be issued at the foregoing rate, twice per week, in lieu of beans or peas, or in lieu of rice or hominy. Fresh beef may be issued as often as the commanding officer of any detachment or regiment may require it, when practicable, in place of salt meat."*

NOTE.—"After the present insurrection shall cease, the ration shall be as provided by law and regulations on the first day of July, eighteen hundred and sixty-one." (Section 13, Act approved August 3, 1861.) To wit, as follows:—

"The ration is three-fourths of a pound of pork or bacon, or one and a fourth pound of fresh or salt beef; eighteen ounces of bread or flour, or twelve ounces of hard bread, or one and a fourth pound of corn meal; and at the rate, to one hundred rations, of eight quarts of beans, or in lieu thereof, ten pounds of rice, or in lieu thereof, twice per week, one hundred and fifty ounces of desiccated potatoes, and one hundred ounces of mixed vegetables; ten pounds of coffee, or in lieu thereof, one and one-half pound of tea; fifteen pounds of sugar; four quarts of vinegar; one pound of sperm candles, or one and one-fourth pound of adamantine candles, or one and one-half pound of tallow candles; four pounds of soap, and two quarts of salt."†

---

* New Regulations of Subsistence Department, 1862.
† Revised Army Reg. 1861, Art. XLIII. ¿ 1191.

According to existing laws, therefore, the ration for the duration of the rebellion may be tabulated as follows :—

Articles.		For one man.		For 100 men.
Either may be drawn, or a part of each. Thus, of 100 rations, 60 may be fresh beef, and 40 pork or bacon.	Pork............... Bacon..............	¾ lb.	Daily.	75 lbs.
	Salt beef.......... Fresh beef......	1¼ lb.	Daily.	125 lbs.
Either may be drawn, or a part o each.	Bread .... Flour...............	22 oz.	Daily.	137½ lbs.
	Hard bread.......	1 lb.	Daily.	100 lbs.
Either...................	Rice.................	1.6 oz.	Daily.	10 lbs.
	Beans..............	0.64 gills.	Daily.	8 quarts.
May be substituted for rice or beans, if desired.	Desiccated potatoes............	1.5 oz.	Bi-weekly.	9 lbs. 6 oz.
	Desic'ted mixed vegetables.....	1 oz.	Bi-weekly.	6 lbs. 4 oz.
If practicable............	Potatoes...........	1 lb.	Tri-weekly.	100 lbs.
Tea may be substituted for coffee, on requisition of the proper officer.	Coffee..............	1.6 oz.	Daily.	10 lbs.
	Tea..................	0.24 oz.	Daily.	1 lb. 8 oz.
	Sugar...............	2.4 oz.	Daily.	15 lbs.
	Vinegar............	0.32 gills.	Daily.	4 quarts.
Either	Sperm candles...	0.16 oz.	Daily.	1 lb.
	Adamantine candles	0.20 oz.	Daily.	1¼ lbs.
	Tallow candles..	0.24 oz.	Daily.	1½ lbs.
	Soap	0.64 oz.	Daily.	4 lbs.
	Salt..................	0.16 gills.	Daily.	2 quarts.

Occasional issues (extra) of molasses are made of two quarts to one hundred rations. Peas or hominy are sometimes issued instead of rice or beans. The following table shows the quantities in bulk of each article in from 1 to 100,000 rations :

THE HOSPITAL STEWARD'S MANUAL.

Table showing the Quantity in Bulk of any

NUMBER OF RATIONS.	PORK.			BEEF.		FLOUR.		BEANS OR PEAS.		RICE, HOMINY, AND *GREEN COFFEE.		TEA.	
	Barrels.	Pounds.	Ounces.	Pounds.	Ounces.	Barrels.	Pounds.	Ounces.	Bushels.	Quarts.	Gills.	Pounds.	Ounces.	Pounds.	Ounces.
1	......	......	12	1	4	......	1	6	......	......	0.64	......	1.6	......	0.24
2	......	1	8	2	8	......	2	12	......	......	1.28	......	3.2	......	0.48
3	......	2	4	3	12	......	4	2	......	......	1.92	......	4.8	......	0.72
4	......	3	......	5	......	......	5	8	......	......	2.56	......	6.4	......	0.96
5	......	3	12	6	4	......	6	14	......	......	3.20	......	8.0	......	1.20
6	......	4	8	7	8	......	8	4	......	......	3.84	......	9.6	......	1.44
7	......	5	4	8	12	......	9	10	......	......	4.48	......	11.2	......	1.68
8	......	6	......	10	......	......	11	......	......	......	5.12	......	12.8	......	1.92
9	......	6	12	11	4	......	12	6	......	......	5.76	......	14.4	......	2.16
10	......	7	8	12	8	......	13	12	......	......	6.40	1	......	......	2.4
20	......	15	......	25	......	......	27	8	......	1	4.60	2	......	......	4.8
30	......	22	8	37	8	......	41	4	......	2	3.20	3	......	......	7.2
40	......	30	......	50	......	......	55	......	......	3	1.60	4	......	......	9.6
50	......	37	8	62	8	......	68	12	......	4	......	5	......	......	12.0
60	......	45	......	75	......	......	82	8	......	4	6.40	6	......	......	14.4
70	......	52	8	87	8	......	96	4	......	5	4.80	7	......	1	0.8
80	......	60	......	100	......	......	110	......	......	6	3.20	8	......	1	3.2
90	......	67	8	112	8	......	123	12	......	7	1.60	9	......	1	5.6
100	......	75	......	125	......	......	137	8	......	8	......	10	......	1	8.0
1,000	3	150	......	1,250	......	7	3	......	2	16	......	100	......	15	......
10,000	37	100	......	12,500	......	70	30	......	25	......	......	1,000	......	150	......
100,000	375	......	......	125,000	......	701	104	......	250	......	......	10,000	......	1500	......

NOTE.—Fresh potatoes are issued, three times per week, at one pound to the ration; fresh flour, when on hand for issue, 12½ pounds to the 100 rations *in lieu* of beans or peas; molasses, one

* *Roasted* or *ground* coffee is issued at the rate of *eight* pounds to the 100 rations.

† *Sperm* candles are issued at the rate of *one* pound, and *tallow* candles at the rate of *one pound*

THE HOSPITAL STEWARD'S MANUAL. 161

Number of Rations, from 1 to 100,000.

SUGAR.		VINEGAR AND MOLASSES.		ADAMANTINE CANDLES.		SOAP.		SALT.		DESICCATED POTATOES.		MIXED VEGETABLES.	
Pounds.	Ounces.	Gallons.	Quarts.	Gills.	Pounds.	Ounces.	Pounds.	Ounces.	Bushels.	Quarts.	Gills.	Pounds.	Ounces.	Pounds.	Ounces.
....	2.4	......	......	0.32	......	0.2	......	0.64	......	......	0.16	....	1.5	....	1
....	4.8	......	......	0.64	......	0.4	......	1.28	......	......	0.32	....	3.0	....	2
....	7.2	......	......	0.96	......	0.6	......	1.92	......	......	0.48	....	4.5	....	3
....	9.6	......	......	1.28	......	0.8	......	2.56	......	......	0.64	....	6.0	....	4
....	12.0	......	......	1.60	......	1.0	......	3.20	......	......	0.80	....	7.5	....	5
....	14.4	......	......	1.92	......	1.2	......	3.84	......	......	0.96	....	9.0	....	6
1	0.8	......	......	2.24	......	1.4	......	4.48	......	......	1.12	....	10.5	....	7
1	3.2	......	......	2.56	......	1.6	......	5.12	......	......	1.28	....	12.0	....	8
1	5.6	......	......	2.88	......	1.8	......	5.76	......	......	1.44	....	13.5	....	9
1	8.0	......	......	3.20	......	2.	......	6.40	......	......	1.60	....	15.0	....	10
3	......	......	......	6.40	......	4.	......	12.80	......	......	3.20	1	14.0	1	4
4	8.0	......	1	1.60	......	6.	1	3.20	......	......	4.80	2	13.0	1	14
6	......	......	1	4.80	......	8.	1	9.60	......	......	6.40	3	12.0	2	8
7	8.0	......	2	......	......	10.	2	......	......	1	....	4	11.0	3	2
9	......	......	2	3.20	......	12.	......	6.40	......	1	1.60	5	10.0	3	12
10	8.0	......	2	6.40	......	14.	2	12.80	......	1	3.20	6	9.0	4	6
12	......	......	3	1.60	1	......	3	3.20	......	1	4.80	7	8.0	5	......
13	8.0	......	3	4.80	1	2.	3	9.60	......	1	6.40	8	7.0	5	10
15	......	1	......	......	1	4.	4	......	......	2	....	9	6.0	6	4
150	......	10	......	......	12	8.	40	......	......	20	....	93	12.0	62	8
1,500	......	100	......	......	125	......	400	......	6	8	....	937	8.0	625	......
15,000	......	1000	......	......	1250	......	4000	......	62	16	....	9,375	......	6,250	......

onions, when on hand for issue, three bushels *in lieu* of one bushel of beans or peas; bean gallon to the 100 rations, twice per week.

and a half, to the 100 rations.

14*

SECTION III.—OF PROVISION RETURNS.

Provisions are drawn for the hospital from the commissary on a provision return,* blank forms for which are furnished by the commissary for that purpose.

It should represent the total quantity of each article to which the hospital is entitled, the quantity of each actually drawn, and the quantity of each retained by the commissary, which is to be credited to the hospital by him.

The provision return must be signed by the surgeon in charge, and by the commanding officer having authority to direct the issue.

The following is the form:—

---

* Form 13, Subsistence Depart., Revised Reg., p. 267.

Provision Return of the General Hospital at ———, for ——— days, commencing the ——— day of ———, 186—, and ending the ——— day of ———, 186—.

STATION.	RATIONS OF—					REMARKS.
		Retained.	Total actually drawn.	Total rations due...		
	Number of Men.					
	Number of Women.					
	Total.					
	Number of Days.					
	Number of Rations.					
	Pork.					
	Salt Beef.					
	Fresh Beef.					
	Flour.					
	Beans.					
	Rice.					
	Coffee.					
	Tea.					
	Sugar.					
	Vinegar.					
	Sperm Candles.					
	Adamant. Candles.					
	Soap.					
	Salt.					
	Potatoes.					
	Molasses.					
	&c.					Here specify the number of cadets, stewards, female nurses, guards, attendants, patients, and total.

The A. C. S. will issue on the above return.

————, *Commanding Officer.*

————, *Surgeon U. S. A.*

NOTES.—This return will embrace only the *actual* number present in hospital, including the sick, stewards, attendants, and all entitled to a ration. Returns for hospital matrons will be made separately, mentioning the name of each matron.

The provision return is made out by the hospital steward, and is based upon his knowledge of the actual needs of the hospital: some experience is needed to enable him to draw the proper quantity of each article, and no absolute rule can be laid down, as the amount needed will vary to a considerable extent, in accordance with the proportion of severe cases of disease or injury in the hospital. In all doubtful cases it is better to draw too much than too little; for the *patients must never be stinted* in any thing for the sake of making hospital fund, and, if there is a surplus, so much less may be drawn on the next return. After having made out the provision return, it is carried by the hospital steward to the surgeon for his approval and signature, and afterwards to the commanding officer.

The return, having been approved, is carried by the steward with the hospital wagon to the commissary, the provisions obtained and brought to the hospital.

Duplicate copies of the provision returns should be kept on file by the steward, in order that they may be compared with the monthly statement of the hospital fund, furnished by the commissary to the surgeon.

At all posts where there is an army bakery, it is usual for the hospital to draw bread instead of flour. This is effected as follows:— When drawing the ration, the steward receives from the commissary an order for the number of rations of bread his provision return calls for; one ration of flour being regarded as the equivalent of a ration of bread, weight for weight. The steward carries the order to the bakery and receives the bread. Where the bakery bakes daily, it is usual for the steward to draw each day only the number of loaves required for the following twenty-four hours, instead of drawing the whole amount at once.

In like manner, when fresh beef is drawn, the steward does not generally receive the fresh beef from the commissary, but an order for it, which he carries to the shamble, designated by the commissary, and there receives the beef. In warm weather the steward should not draw at once the whole amount, but, learning the days on which animals are butchered, should procure each butchering-day the portion necessary to last to the next. If butchering is done daily, the meat should be procured daily, using each day meat killed the day before.

SECTION IV.—OF HOSPITAL STORES.

Besides what can be obtained from the commissary, certain articles needed for the diet of the sick are obtained from the *medical purveyor*, under the title of hospital stores. These articles are enumerated in "regulations" as arrow-root, barley, cinnamon, cloves, cocoa, farina, ground Jamaica ginger, nutmegs, tea, whiskey, and wine.

These articles are obtained by requisitions on the medical purveyor, made by the surgeon and approved by the medical director or the Surgeon-General, in accordance with the regulations which will be hereafter described under the head of "*Requisitions for Medical and Hospital Supplies.*"

SECTION V.—OF PURCHASES FOR THE HOSPITAL.

All articles needed for the subsistence of the sick in hospital, which cannot be obtained from the commissary or the medical purveyor, are purchased out of the hospital fund, out of which are also purchased all such other articles needed for the *comfort* of the sick as are not authorized to be obtained in any other way.

Purchases for the subsistence of the sick may be divided into two classes.

First, purchases necessary to complete the ordinary "*full diet table*," as adopted by the surgeon in charge for his hospital, such as milk, butter, fresh vegetables, *e.g.* cabbage, onions, turnips, &c., mustard, pepper, dried fruit, sour-krout, and all similar articles. Ice comes also under this head.

Secondly, purchases necessary for the "*extra diet*" ordered by the surgeon in special cases, such as eggs, oysters, chickens, fresh fruit, oranges, lemons, malt liquors, &c. &c.

These articles will be referred to hereafter, in connection with the question of "*Diet and Cooking.*"

Purchases for the comfort of the sick may include a great variety of articles, as purchases of oil, or expenditures for gas for lighting the hospital, hospital furniture which cannot be obtained by requisition on the medical purveyor, as window-shades, water-coolers, &c.&c., printed blanks for passes, discharges, labels, printed rules and regulations, &c. &c.

The authority for making these purchases

is granted in regulations in the following terms:—

"The *hospital fund*, or any portion of it, may be expended by the commissary, on the requisition of the medical officer, in the purchase of any article for the subsistence or comfort of the sick, not authorized to be otherwise furnished."*

Practically, the purchases for the diet of the hospital are generally made for large general hospitals in the following manner:—

A purveyor for the hospital is designated by the surgeon in charge. The purveyor should, if possible, be some respectable produce-dealer in the neighborhood of the hospital. Each morning, or as often as necessary, the steward makes out a list of the articles needed, obtains the approval of the surgeon in charge, and sends it to the dealer, who procures the articles and sends them to the hospital. A special memorandum-book should be kept by the steward, in which he should keep copies of these lists for comparison with the articles actually furnished on their arrival, as well as for comparison with the monthly bill. It will be

---

* Revised Reg., Art. XLIII. ¿ 1195.

found most economical to make purchases of all articles not immediately perishable in sufficiently large quantities to obtain the advantage of wholesale price. At the end of the month a bill is made out in duplicate, and approved by the medical officer in charge, according to the following form :—

170 THE HOSPITAL STEWARD'S MANUAL.

The United States
   To .... Dr.

186 .		Dolls.	Cts.
	$		

I certify, on honor, that the above-specified articles were purchased on my requisition for the use of the sick in hospital under my charge.

....

.... *Surgeon* ....

Received at .... this .... day of ...., 186—, from Lieut. ...., A.C.S., U.S.A., ...Dollars and .... Cents, in full of the above account.

....

  (SIGNED IN DUPLICATE.)

  NOTES.—" No officer or agent in the military service shall purchase from *any other person* in the military service."
  Purchases for a hospital from subsistence funds may be made by a commissary *to the extent only* of the " hospital fund" due such hospital, and must be limited to articles " for the subsistence or comfort of the sick *not authorized to be otherwise furnished.*"
  Medicines, regular supplies of the Quartermaster's Department, &c. &c., must not be obtained from the hospital fund.

This duplicate bill, duly approved, is given to the dealer, who receipts it, presents it to the commissary, and receives the money.

Printed blanks for this purpose can usually be obtained from the commissary.

Milk for the hospital is usually best obtained from some respectable dealer in that article, to be designated by the surgeon in charge. He should be paid monthly, in the manner above described. Ice for the hospital should likewise be procured, when possible, from an ice-dealer, who should furnish daily the required quantity, and be paid in the same manner.

If any of the articles thus purchased be furnished of inferior quality, or if the quantity be not fully that agreed upon and charged, or if the charges exceed the market-price of any article, the circumstance should be reported at once by the steward to the surgeon in charge, who will take such action as the circumstances of the case demand.

Too much care cannot be exercised by the steward in this particular. All articles received should be at once compared with his memorandum-book, and, if any doubt exist as to the quantity of any thing, it should be at once weighed or measured. Milk should be received in vessels of uniform size, and, if not received by the steward in person, the attendant charged with that duty should be instructed to report to the steward, daily, immediately after its receipt, whether the quantity is correct and the quality good. Any reported deficiency should be at once investigated by the steward, and, if found to exist, should be immediately reported to the surgeon.

Unless this is done, the hospital is liable to constant imposition.

SEC. VI.—THE HOSPITAL FUND—ITS MANAGEMENT.

The management of the provision returns, and of the purchases for the hospital, is an important and responsible part of the duties of the hospital steward. If it be carefully performed, the hospital fund will be found, under ordinary circumstances, more than adequate for all the necessities of the hospital,—so much so that it is directed in regulations, that,

" At large depots or general hospitals, this fund may be partly expended for the benefit of dependent posts or detachments, on requisitions approved by the medical director or senior surgeon of the district." And that, on the first of January, each year, one-fourth of every "hospital fund," if less than $150, and one-half if more, will be dropped by the commissary from the fund, and will be paid over to the treasurer of the Soldiers' Home by the Commissary-General.

Other purchases for the hospital than those for the diet of the patients should be made only on the direction of the surgeon, and are to be paid for in the same manner.

The steward should keep on file copies of all these bills, for comparison with the "monthly statement of the hospital fund."

Under certain circumstances the commissary has been authorized by the Commissary-General to pay over the hospital fund in money to the surgeon for expenditure. This course is objectionable, as the surgeon becomes thus responsible for public money, and is burdened with the preparation of all the returns and vouchers required by regulations of disbursing officers.

A copy of the monthly statement of the hospital fund is to be made by the steward from the abstract presented by the commissary for the signature of the surgeon in charge. This should be done as soon as practicable after the close of the month, in the following form:—

174 THE HOSPITAL STEWARD'S MANUAL.

A Monthly Statement of the Hospital Fund at ———, for the month of ———, 186—.

					Dolls.	Cts.
Dr.						
To balance due hospital last month......................................					10	00
493 rations, being whole amount due this month, at 15 cents per ration...					73	95
Cr.	ISSUED.			Dolls.	Cts.	83	95
By the following provisions, at contract prices:						
37½ pounds of Pork.................at 6 cents per lb...			2	25		
93¾ pounds of Salt Beef............at 8 cents per lb...			7	50		
218¾ pounds of Fresh Beef..........at 4 cents per lb...			8	75		
233¾ pounds of Flour...............at 4 cents per lb...			9	35		
75 pounds of Hard Bread............at 5 cents per lb...			3	75		
¾ bushel of Beans..................at 7 cts. per bush...				84		
10 pounds of Rice..................at 5 cents per lb...				50		
18 pounds of Coffee................at 15 cents per lb...			2	70		
¾ pound of Tea.....................at 48 cents per lb...				36		
30¾ pounds of Sugar................at 8 cents per lb...			2	36		
6¾ quarts of Vinegar...............at 4 cents per qt...				27		
⅞ pound of Sperm Candles..........at 40 cents per lb...				35		
3 pounds of Adamantine Candles.at 20 cents per lb...				60		
5 pounds of Soap...................at 6¼ cents per lb...				32		
3¼ quarts of Salt..................at 2 cents per qt...				6		
PURCHASED.		Dolls.	Cts.				
2 pairs of chickens, at 25 cents each...........	1	00				
2 dozen eggs, at 18 cents per dozen.............		36				
2 brooms, at 25 cents each......................		50				
4 tin pans, at 12½ cents each..................		50				
4 quarts of milk, at 7 cents per quart.........		28				
3 dozen oranges, at 25 cents per dozen.......		75				
Total issued and expended............	3	39	40	06	43	45
Balance due this month...					40	50

——— ———, *Surgeon* ———.

A copy of the monthly "statement of the hospital fund" must be filed among the records of the hospital, and a copy furnished to the surgeon in charge to transmit to the Surgeon-General.*

The amount of the hospital fund will vary under different circumstances, and the theory is that, ordinarily, it will vary with the wants of the hospital. Thus, if the hospital contains a large proportion of serious cases, there will be a great saving on the ration, and a large hospital fund, on which the drafts for extra diets and other comforts for the sick will be proportionately large. If, on the other hand, the hospital principally contains convalescents, there will be comparatively little saving on the ration, and consequently a small hospital fund, but, at the same time, the necessities for extras to be purchased will also be comparatively small.

Two causes, however, will be found to influence the hospital fund, besides the character of the cases in the hospital. The first is the cost-price of the ration at the post; the second is the economy with which the purchases

---

* Revised Reg., Art. XLIV. § 1264.

for the hospital and the hospital-kitchen are managed. As to the first cause, it is very evident that the amount of saving in dollars will be much larger at a post where the ration is estimated at twenty-two cents, than where it is estimated at fifteen cents. But, practically, it will be found that this cause does not materially influence the amount of purchases that can be made with the hospital fund, for where the cost-price of the ration is small, there will generally be found cheap markets for the purchase of the extras needed, and, on the contrary, dear markets where the cost-price of the ration is high.

The chief cause, therefore, practically, which influences the size of the hospital fund in its relation to the actual wants of the hospital, will be found to be the economy displayed in the administration of the hospital. Economy is secured by keeping the provisions and stores of the hospital under lock and key, so as to prevent all unauthorized expenditure; by keeping a strict account of all authorized expenditures, and comparing from time to time the daily expenditures with each other and the number of patients, so as to become at once aware of any inadvertent extravagance; by prudence in drawing or purchasing perishable articles, such as fresh meat, &c., which should be so managed that, while there is enough for all purposes, none should be left over to spoil; by skill and economy in the management of the kitchen; (on the whole, it may be said that bad cooking is more extravagant than good cooking, requiring larger quantities of ingredients, and giving worse results;) by economy with the gas, lamps, or other means resorted to to light the hospital; and, finally, by taking care to make the purchases for the hospital of honest dealers, and to pay for them no more than the market-price. Twenty-five to fifty per cent. of the hospital fund, or even more, may be lost by making the purchases of an improper person.

The hospital fund, in a properly managed hospital, should amount to from one-fourth to one-half of the total cost of the rations to which the number of patients and attendants in the hospital are entitled.

Thus, in a hospital for five hundred patients, at a post where the ration is estimated at eighteen cents cost-price for each full ration, the monthly savings should be at least $650, and, under favorable circumstances, may swell to

$1400, or even more. When a hospital is first established, the whole of this sum should not be expended, the excess of savings over expenditures being allowed to accumulate till it forms a sum at least as large as the monthly savings, after which there need never be any hesitation in expending each month, for the comfort of the sick, all the savings of the month previous.

That the above estimate is not excessive may be proved by a single example from among many. In the Seminary Hospital, Georgetown, D.C., under the efficient management of Assistant Surgeon (now Surgeon) J. R. Smith, U.S.A., during the year subsequent to its establishment, in July, 1861, the number of patients was from one hundred and thirty to one hundred and fifty, the average cost-price of the ration eighteen cents, and the monthly savings from $350 to $450. The average monthly expenditures, after the first few months, were about the same; the balance due the hospital at the close of each month, on the monthly statement of the hospital fund, from $300 to $500.

This would correspond to a monthly saving

of nearly $1500 in a hospital for five hundred patients.

The same favorable results have been obtained elsewhere whenever due economy and care have been employed in the management.

SECTION VII.—OF THE CARE OF PROVISIONS AND HOSPITAL STORES.

Hospital stores, and those parts of the ration which are not speedily perishable, such as coffee, sugar, beans, rice, &c. &c., should be kept by the steward, when possible, in a storeroom, under lock and key. The store-room should be properly shelved, and the articles should be stored in a systematic and orderly manner. The strictest cleanliness is necessary, and boxes and barrels should be kept covered to exclude dust and dirt.

Fresh meat, fresh fruit and vegetables, and the like perishable articles should be kept in a separate place. In all large hospitals a pantry should be specially set aside for this purpose, in which during the summer-time the ice should also be kept. Where the hospital is not large enough to require a separate room or building for this purpose, a family refrigerator, of a size proportioned to the necessities of the case, may be purchased, by direction of the surgeon, out of the hospital fund, and will answer the purpose excellently. The pantry or refrigerator, like the store-room, should be kept locked.

The hospital steward is responsible to the surgeon for the proper care and economical use of the provisions and hospital supplies. This is especially enjoined in regulations, which provide that the senior medical officer of a hospital "will require the steward to take due care of the hospital stores and supplies; to enter in a book, daily, the issues to the ward-masters, cooks, and nurses; to prepare the provision returns, and receive and distribute the rations."

The book here directed should be ruled in accordance with the form prescribed by regulations.* It should be kept in the store-room, and each article entered at the time of issue. The following is the form prescribed:—

---

* Med. Regulations, Form 6.

DATE.	Lbs. Rice.	Lbs. Sugar.	Oz. Tea.	Qts. Wine.	Qts. Brandy.	Lbs. Coffee.	&c. &c.	&c. &c.	&c. &c.	REMARKS.

Account of Hospital Stores, Furniture, &c., issued.

The book should be ruled so as to give a column to each article kept on hand, and leave a few blank columns over for extras.

Issues should be made daily, at some definite and convenient hour. Articles needed for the ration should be issued to the cook, or, in a large general hospital, to the hospital steward having charge of the kitchen. Where there is more than one kitchen, the steward or cook having charge of each should receive his share separately, and each should be charged with it separately upon the steward's book.

Issues of hospital stores upon the extra-diet list, or of liquors, are to be charged to the nurse who receives them. The stewards, cooks, and nurses receiving these articles are responsible to the chief steward for their proper use and distribution.

CHAPTER II.

Of the Diet Table.

UNDER direction of the surgeon, a regular diet table should be established in every hospital. For convenience' sake, the diet should be divided into three classes,—full, half, and low,—which are to be designated in the diet and prescription book by the letters F., H., and L. In prescribing daily for each patient, the surgeon is directed in the medical regulations to write, with the prescription for each, one of these letters, to indicate which class of diet he shall have. The steward is therefore able, by consulting the record, to know at once how many patients, daily, each class of diet is to be prepared for.

To these three classes of diet must be added the articles of *extra diet*, including liquors, which must be specially ordered daily by the surgeon for each patient requiring them.

SECTION I.—OF FULL DIET.

To establish a proper diet table for hospital patients requiring full diet, is a problem which still exercises the best abilities of scientific dietitians, and the discussion of which it is not possible to enter into in this place. The actual problem presented to the hospital steward in this country is to utilize to the utmost extent the articles of diet which he can obtain from the commissary and medical purveyor, and those which the surgeon authorizes him to purchase with the hospital fund.

With proper care in the management of the hospital fund, it is possible to make these supplies of such a character that the diet of a United States military hospital may readily be made equal or superior to that of any of the hospitals in the world.

To do this, greater care than hitherto must be exercised in the purchases, in the arrangement of the diet table, and especially in the *cooking*, of our military hospitals.

There should be three meals daily.

Breakfast at six o'clock during the summer and seven during the winter months.

Dinner at twelve o'clock during the summer and half-past twelve in the winter months.

Supper at six.

Breakfast should consist of well-made *coffee*, of reasonable strength, with *milk and sugar*, of *bread and butter*, and of some *relish*, which should vary daily.

The *coffee* should be made according to the receipt hereafter given, and should have the milk and sugar added to it in the kitchen. One pint should be served to each patient. Pains should be taken to have it well made and served hot.

Half an ounce of *butter* should be served to each patient.

A slice of *bread*, of about six ounces' weight, should be laid by each plate; but the patients should not be limited to this quantity.

A dozen additional slices, of about three ounces each, may be placed in plates, at convenient intervals, along the table of the mess-room, and each one allowed to help himself according to his appetite. This plan will be found more economical, as well as more satisfactory, than the plan of adopting a fixed ration—say eight ounces—and giving it to each patient irrespective of his appetite. In this case, while certain patients are not satisfied, and complain that they are stinted, the great majority waste a portion of their share.

The *relish* should consist of either cold meat, bacon, or meat stew with onions or potatoes, salt or fresh fish, or any similar article, which may be directed by the surgeon to be placed upon the diet table. Each patient should have his share of the breakfast relish put upon his plate. About four ounces of cold meat, eight ounces of hash or meat stew, eight ounces of codfish hash, four ounces of salt or four ounces of fresh fish, are proper quantities for each patient.

It is advised that but a single relish be provided for the whole full diet list for any one day, and that in the diet table for a week the relish be different upon each day,—the principle of the importance of *variety*, as well as quantity and nutritive value, in a diet, having been fully established in past experience.

Receipts for preparing several dishes suitable for breakfast relishes will be given in the chapter on cooking.*

Dinner presents a more difficult problem, and one which must be met by the surgeon in

---

* Part III. chap. iv.

charge in accordance with the possibilities of each hospital locality.

In a general way, it may be said that the dinner should consist of some well-made soup, of meat, and of vegetables. Bread in slices of two or three ounces each should be put upon the table, that each patient who wishes may eat one or more slices with his soup. Beef soup is the most generally available, as beef is the only fresh meat at present issued by the commissary. But mutton soup, and, in some hospital locations, chicken soup, may be advantageously substituted by drawing so much less beef from the commissary, and purchasing the mutton or fowls with the hospital fund.

Good vegetable soup may be made without using any *fresh* meat, thus allowing the fresh meat for the day to be baked or roasted. A number of receipts for different forms of soup will be found in the article on cooking.

Too much pains cannot be bestowed in seeing that the soup is well made, as its nutritive value, as well as its palatability, depends to a great extent on the mode in which it is prepared.

About a pint and a half of soup may be served to each patient at dinner.

Once or twice a week a well-made stew of meat and vegetables, such as onions and potatoes, may be served instead of soup.

The meat from the soup may be served for dinner on certain designated days of the week, but, as this meat is far inferior in nutritive value to meat which has not been thus used, it is a grave error to depend upon it for the daily dinner. On days on which other meat is supplied for dinner, the meat from the soup, when it is made of fresh meat, may be used cold, as a breakfast relish, on the following day, or may be made into a stew for the same purpose, with a little salt meat to give it flavor, and proper quantities of potatoes or onions.

Thus, for example, soup made of fresh meat may be served four days in the week, vegetable soup, as pea or bean soup, made with salt meat, on two days, and meat stew with potatoes and onions on one day.

Roast or baked fresh meat may be served on the same days with the vegetable soup. The meat from the soup may be used on two days at dinner; on two days it may be used cold, or stewed for next day's breakfast, and its place taken at dinner by salt meat, baked or broiled. Fried meat should be avoided as much as possible.

The day meat stew is substituted for soup, some plain pudding should be served.

The quantities of these several articles of diet which should be allowed to each patient may be stated as follows :—

Roast or baked meat, or of boiled meat from the soup, 8 oz. Baked, boiled, or broiled salt meat, 6 oz. Meat stew with onions or potatoes, 1 pint. Pudding, 6 oz.

Potatoes, boiled or roasted, should be served three or four times a week; other vegetables, as turnips boiled, or baked beans, cabbage boiled or raw (cold-slaugh), spinach, sour-krout, &c., on other days. The quantity should be for each patient at each meal about eight ounces of potatoes or of other vegetables.

It is believed by the author of this work that a pint of some mild malt liquor might advantageously, and without too great expense, be added to the dinner of a general hospital in most localities. To do this, however, the malt liquor (ale, or lager-bier) should be purchased by the cask or casks, and drawn as needed, bottled malt liquors being much more expensive, without being better. This is, however, a subject which must be determined in every general hospital by the state of the hospital fund and the views of the surgeon in charge.

Supper should consist of well-made tea, not too strong, served, like the coffee at breakfast, with milk and sugar: one pint should be allowed to each patient, with bread and butter in the same quantity as directed for breakfast.

To this may be added, occasionally, well-stewed dried fruit, or the bread and butter may be substituted by a proper allowance of mush and molasses, or mush and milk,—mush one pint, with one pint of milk to each patient, or molasses at the rate of about one gallon to the hundred men, allowing each to help himself according to his taste.

SECTION II.—OF HALF-DIET.

Half-diet is intended for those patients whose condition is such as to require a smaller quantity of nutriment than is afforded by the full diet. The articles entering into its composition, and the quantities of each in any case, will be directed by the surgeon in charge. It should approximate the following conditions:—

Breakfast.—Tea, with milk and sugar, about one pint; bread, not to exceed six ounces; butter, half an ounce.

Dinner.—Similar to full diet, but the quantities smaller, say—

    Soup, ... 1 pint.
    Meat, ... 6 oz.
    Potatoes, or other vegetables, 6 oz.

Supper.—Tea, bread and butter, as for breakfast. Mush and milk, or molasses, may occasionally be substituted for the bread and butter.

SECTION III.—OF LOW DIET.

Low diet is intended for patients requiring still less nutriment, and for whom the soup, meat, and vegetables furnished those on full or half diet would be too difficult of digestion.

The precise composition of the low diet of any hospital will be directed by the surgeon in charge. Some such scale as the following should be approximated:—

Breakfast.—Tea and toast, with or without some form of water-gruel, as directed by the surgeon for individual cases. Say, tea, ¾ pint; bread, toasted, 5 oz., or 3 oz. if gruel is furnished; gruel (oatmeal or other), 1 pint.

Dinner.—Mutton, beef, or chicken broth, 1 pint, with arrow-root, panada, farina, corn-starch, rice pudding, or some similar article.

Supper.—The same as breakfast.

SECTION IV.—OF EXTRA DIET.

Under the head of extra diet may be included extras ordered by the surgeon for patients put upon either of the above diet scales, and those special cases in which, for a particular purpose, a diet entirely unlike either of them is directed.

Extras are most generally ordered for patients whose condition is such that they are put upon low diet. They include eggs, poached, boiled, beaten raw, or otherwise prepared; oysters, raw or cooked; chickens; fresh fruit; custards; jellies, or any similar articles which may be directed by the surgeon. Under this head also may be included malt liquors, wines, and distilled liquors. Liquors may very frequently be advantageously ordered as extras to patients upon half, or even upon full, diet.

In certain cases, however, none of these forms of diet are adapted to the case. Thus, in certain fever cases the diet may be ordered to consist entirely of beef essence, or beef tea, with wine whey, or milk punch, given at stated intervals, or, as in certain wounds about the face interfering with mastication, it may be necessary that the whole diet should be in a liquid form, consisting of soups, gruels, and the like (spoon-diet). These forms of diet must always be specially ordered by the surgeon; and there is hence no necessity of discussing them in detail in this place. A number of receipts for preparing extras of various kinds will be found in the article on cooking.

SECTION V.—SPECIMEN OF DIET-TABLE.

The following diet table is presented as a specimen of what may be effected by reasonable care on the part of the hospital steward when his efforts are directed by a surgeon aware of the resources of the service. It is the diet table actually adopted and carried out in the Seminary Hospital, Georgetown, D.C., under the care of Assistant Surgeon (now Surgeon) J. R. Smith, U.S.A.

The same diet table, with some trifling modifications, has been adopted in the Judiciary Square Hospital (for 250 patients), under direction of Assistant Surgeon (now Medical Inspector) E. P. Vollum, U.S.A.

Diet Table of the Seminary Hospital, Georgetown, D.C., successfully adopted also by the Judiciary Square Hospital, Washington, D.C.

FULL DIET.

		SUNDAY.	MONDAY.	TUESDAY.	WEDNESDAY.	THURSDAY.	FRIDAY.	SATURDAY.
BREAKFAST.		Bread and Butter. Coffee. Cold Meat.	Bread and Butter. Coffee. Hash.	Coffee. Fried Mush and Molasses	Bread and Butter. Coffee. Codfish.	Bread and Butter. Coffee. Hominy.	Bread and Butter. Coffee. Eggs (2 apiece).	Coffee. Fried Mush and Molasses.
DINNER.		Soup. Boiled Meat. Potatoes. Bread Pudding.	Irish Stew. Bread.	Soup. Roast Beef. Vegetables. Bread.	Pork and Beans. Potatoes. Bread Pudding.	Chicken Soup. Potatoes. Bread. Rice.	Mutton Stew. Vegetables. Bread.	Soup. Roast Beef. Potatoes. Bread.
SUPPER.		Bread and Butter. Tea. Dried fruit, stewed.	Coffee. Mush and Milk or Molasses.	Bread and Butter. Tea. Cold Beef.	Bread and Butter. Tea. Dried fruit, stewed.	Bread and Molasses. Coffee. Hash.	Coffee. Mush and Milk or Molasses.	Bread and Butter. Cold Beef.

Another form of diet table is that adopted in the general hospital in West Philadelphia, by Surgeon I. I. Hayes, U.S.V.

In this form the several articles which *may* be had for each meal are printed. Each day the surgeon in charge fills up the diet table for the next day, indicating the articles to be used for each meal by drawing a line through those not selected, and writing opposite each article the number of rations to be issued, and the quantity in bulk of the materials to be employed. The form is sufficiently comprehensive to explain itself. It is especially adapted to large hospitals, such as that in West Philadelphia, which is intended for over 2000 patients.

196   THE HOSPITAL STEWARD'S MANUAL.

Diet Table of United States Army General

	FULL DIET. No. of Rations.	Quantity in bulk.	HALF DIET. No. of Rations.	Quantity in bulk.
BREAKFAST.	Fresh Beef, Pork, Ham, Mutton, Butter, Milk, Bread, Coffee, Sugar, Molasses, Hash,		Bread or Toast, Milk, Sugar, Tea, Butter,	
DINNER.	Soup, Fresh Beef, Corned Beef, Pork, Mutton, Beans, Potatoes, Vegetables, Hominy, Rice, Mush, Pudding, Bread, Mustard,		Soup, Vegetables, Hominy, Rice, Mush, Pudding, Bread,	
SUPPER.	Fresh Beef, Bread, Mush, Milk, Butter, Cheese, Molasses, Sauce, Sugar, Tea,		Bread, Butter, Cheese, Mush, Milk, Sugar, Molasses, Sauce, Tea,	

THE HOSPITAL STEWARD'S MANUAL. 197

Hospital, West Philadelphia, Pa., for ———— 186—.

LOW DIET. No. of Rations.	Quantity in bulk.	EXTRA DIET. No. of Rations.	No. of each.	Quantity in bulk.
Bread, half, Gruel, Barley Water, Tea, Sugar, Milk,		Mutton Broth, Beef Essence, Eggs, Butter, Milk, Tea, Sugar, Mutton, Chickens, Oysters, Pudding, Crackers, Butter, Sugar, Tea, Wine Whey, Milk Punch, Porter, Cocoa, Tea,		
Bread, Butter, Rice, Arrow-Root, Gruel, Barley Water, Cocoa, Tea, Sugar, Milk,				
Gruel, Arrow-Root, Rice Water, Tea, Sugar, Milk,				

17*

(DIET TABLE OF U.S.-ARMY HOSPITAL, WEST PHILADELPHIA.)—Continued.
Consolidated Table of Quantities.

By order of I. I. HAYES, Surgeon in Charge.

		BREAKFAST				DINNER				SUPPER			
		Full, Half, Low, Extra,			Total,	Full, Half, Low, Extra,			Total,	Full, Half, Low, Extra,			Total,	Aggregate,
Crackers.	lbs.												
Oatmeal.	lbs.												
Green Tea.	lbs.												
Black Tea.	lbs.												
Coffee.	lbs.												
Cocoa.	lbs.												
Cheese.	lbs.												
Milk.	qts.												
Butter.	lbs.												
Mustard.	lbs.												
Vegetables.	lbs.												
Molasses.	qts.												
Sugar.	lbs.												
Vinegar.	qts.												
Salt.	qts.												
Potatoes.	pks.												
Bread.	lbs.												
Flour.	lbs.												
Corn Meal.	pks.												
Arrow-Root.	lbs.												
Barley.	lbs.												
Hominy.	lbs.												
Rice.	lbs.												
Peas.	pks.												
Beans.	pks.												
Oysters.	qts.												
Eggs.	doz.												
Chickens.	lbs.												
Ham.	lbs.												
Mutton.	lbs.												
Corned Beef.	lbs.												
Fresh Beef.	lbs.												
Pork.	lbs.												

It is believed that in all general and post hospitals, except those on the western frontier, a scale of diet similar and equal to that above discussed may be maintained. For frontier posts, however, no absolute rules can be laid down. The surgeon of the post soon becomes familiar with the resources of the locality, and, having done so, the best diet scale should be adopted which the possibilities of the case will admit of. All possible gradations will be found, from posts at which fresh vegetables and fresh meat of all kinds can be obtained at prices so low that the hospital fund can procure all the surgeon may desire, with even greater facility than in or near great cities, to posts at which it is almost impossible to procure any provisions except commissary stores and hospital stores, and in which, consequently, the diet can be made very little better than it should be in the regimental hospitals of troops engaged in an actual campaign.

The possibilities of the diet table in the field hospitals of regiments or detachments engaged in marches or campaigns are, of course, much more limited than in the case of general or post hospitals. Where troops are camped for a considerable length of time in the neighborhood of great cities, as happened, for example, to the army of the Potomac during the fall and winter of 1861-62, it is possible and desirable to create a hospital fund, and purchase milk, butter, eggs, fresh vegetables, and other articles of diet for the use of such patients as the surgeon desires to treat in the camp hospital. Where, however, the troops are engaged in marches and the labors of active campaigns, this will generally be found impracticable, and the steward will usually be directed by the surgeon to draw the full ration, and to utilize it and such hospital stores as are furnished by the medical purveyor for field service to the utmost extent.

The problem presented to the steward in these cases is a much more difficult one than in the case of post or general hospitals, and one in which he must constantly call upon the surgeon for advice. The following principles may, however, be laid down for his guidance:

Wherever regular cooking is possible, and the full ration can be drawn, an attempt should be made to comply with the following diet table, or with some similar table prepared for the steward by the surgeon:—

SECTION VI.—DIET TABLE FOR FIELD HOSPITALS.

Full diet table for a field hospital, where the hospital is wholly dependent on the Commissary and the "hospital stores."

Breakfast.—Tea or coffee, 1 pint, with sugar, but without milk. Soft bread, 8 oz. if furnished, or 6 oz. of hard bread, which may be served dry, or prepared by soaking and stewing.

Dinner.—Soup, made of fresh meat, if it is supplied; if not, of salt meat. Beans or peas may be used in making the soup, or a very excellent and palatable soup may be made of the desiccated vegetables which form a part of the ration. (See receipts.) The *meat* to be served with the soup. Where fresh potatoes are issued, *meat stew* may be occasionally served instead of the soup and meat, or the soup may be omitted, and the meat roasted or broiled.

Supper.—The same as breakfast.

Half-diet.—The same as full diet, but with a smaller allowance of soup and meat.

Low diet.—Breakfast and supper, the same; meat broth for dinner, or, instead, arrow-root, farina, or boiled rice.

Where the condition of the patient is such as to require other diet, or extras, he should be sent to the general hospital at the base of operations. When, from the nature of the service, it is not possible to cook regularly, or to draw the full ration, it is best not to attempt to treat in the field those who are sick enough to enter hospital at all, but to send them at once to the general hospitals in the rear.

Directions for cooking in the field will be given in the next chapter (Section III.).

CHAPTER III.

Of the Kitchen and its Management.

SECTION I.—GENERAL MANAGEMENT OF THE KITCHEN.

The kitchen, like every other part of the general hospital, is under the orders of the chief steward, who is responsible to the surgeon for its proper management. The chief cook is, in like manner, responsible to the steward.

It is usual in a large hospital to assign one hospital steward to the exclusive duty of superintending the kitchen. Where this is the case, he is responsible to the chief steward, in the same manner as the cook.

The cooks are hospital attendants, either enlisted men or civilians employed as mentioned in Part I.

According to regulations, one cook is allowed to every thirty patients, which would give ten to a hospital of three hundred men. This number will generally be found more than sufficient for the exigencies of the service.

One of the cooks should be selected by the surgeon as chief cook, and should have charge of the management of all the business of the kitchen. Where a steward is put in charge of the kitchen, the chief cook is responsible to this steward; but where no steward is specially assigned to the kitchen, the chief cook is immediately responsible to the chief steward of the hospital.

It is the business of the steward assigned to the charge of the kitchen of a general hospital, or of the chief cook, where no steward is assigned to the kitchen, to receive from the chief steward the rations and purchases for the diet of each day: he should receive from him, at the same time, the number of full diets, the number of low diets, and the number and kind of extras to be prepared for the day. He should assign the several cooks each to some particular duty, for the execution of which they are to be responsible. He should see that order and discipline are maintained in the kitchen, and that each executes the tasks assigned to him. He should have the receipts adopted in the hospital for soup, for stews, &c., neatly copied upon cards and hung up in some convenient place in the kitchen for the information of those whose duty it is to prepare them. These receipts should only be adopted after due consultation with the surgeon in charge of the hospital, but once selected should be rigidly adhered to.

He should also exercise supervision over the fires, see that they are properly managed, and that no unnecessary waste of fuel occurs.

The kitchen of a general hospital should always be kept perfectly clean and in strict order. Besides the range or stoves, it should have in it one or more large tables for the preparation of articles of diet. Upon the walls should be a sufficient number of shelves to receive the kitchen-utensils, those of each kind having their special places assigned to them, in which they should always be found, except when in use. Order, always indispensable in a kitchen, is especially necessary in that of a large establishment.

The steward or chief cook in charge of the kitchen is responsible that the meals are in readiness at the hours assigned for each, as well as for their quality. The greatest punctuality is demanded on this head. It is also his duty to supervise the distribution of the food from the kitchen. This is effected in various modes, in accordance with the plan of the hospital, which varies in different locations.

Thus, where a general hospital has a single large dining-room for convalescents on full diet, the chief cook issues to the attendants detailed to attend the dining-room the full quantity of coffee, of soup, of bread, &c. prepared for the number of patients allowed by the surgeon to dine at this table. This is carried in bulk to the dining-hall, and there distributed, under the supervision of a responsible attendant, to the several places, before the patients are allowed to enter the room. Where, however, the hospital consists of a number of detached pavilions, each with its own dining-room, he issues to the attendants sent from each, the cooked rations to which the number of patients dining in each are entitled, to be distributed in the same manner.

The diet for patients confined to their beds is distributed on the same general principles. The several articles are issued in bulk to the chief nurse of each ward, or attendants detailed for the purpose, the quantity to be determined by the number of patients allowed each article of diet.

Thus, if in a given ward ten patients are allowed soup according to the full diet table, the steward of the kitchen, or the chief cook, issues fifteen pints of soup to the nurse, who carries it in a suitable vessel to the ward, where it is divided by measure, each patient receiving in the tin cup or soup-dish used for the purpose the quantity allowed him; and so with other articles.

Strict order should be maintained in these issues, and the most careful supervision employed to see that each patient receives his share.

Meat should be divided into rations, and bread cut into slices, before leaving the kitchen.

On no account should patients be allowed to come in person to the kitchen for their rations; nor should they be allowed to visit in the kitchen, where it should invariably be the rule to admit none except those whose business demands their presence.

Whenever it is practicable, it is advisable to have a separate kitchen for the preparation of extras. This kitchen, where female nurses are employed, may generally be put with advantage under the supervision of a competent woman assigned by the surgeon for this duty.

All remarks as to order, punctuality, and cleanliness applied to the general kitchen apply here with equal force.

Cleanliness is indispensable in the kitchen. The floors should be kept dry and well cleaned. The tables should present the strictest propriety, and the utensils should be clean and in good condition. Slops should be received in a large vessel—say a half-hogshead—outside of the kitchen, which should be emptied daily in summer-time, and at least twice a week in winter. Where it is possible to sell these slops, as for feeding pigs, &c., the steward should do so, and use the proceeds as hospital fund.

A few remarks on the mode of maintaining the cleanliness of utensils will not be amiss.

Iron utensils are very generally used for cooking meats. The boilers for soup, the frying-pans, stew-pans, &c., are often of this material. They should be cleaned immediately after using, and before they are put away for the day. Soap or ley should be used to remove the grease, after which they should be carefully dried, as very little moisture will cause them to rust in a short time.

Before using, they should be carefully inspected to see that they are clean, and be rinsed out with a little scalding water. Fine sand may be used with advantage to scour these utensils, especially when they have been rusted.

Iron vessels are sometimes tinned on the interior, and sometimes lined with porcelain. These surfaces will require the same care as in the case of vessels wholly made of these materials respectively.

Copper vessels should never be used in cooking, unless well lined with tin. The lining should be carefully inspected, and renewed whenever the copper begins to show. Grease is to be removed by soap or ley. The copper, as well as the tin lining, may be polished with the finest sand, or with fine brick-dust.

Tin vessels of every kind, after having been cleansed of all grease, may be polished with fine sand or with whiting. Warm water should be used in cleansing tins.

Wooden utensils are also to be kept neat by scouring with the finest sand.

The knives, forks, spoons, plates, cups, and other table-utensils should be thoroughly cleansed and put away after each meal; cooking-utensils, after each time of using. The strictest cleanliness is necessary, and too great care cannot be used to attain this end.

SECTION II.—OF FIRES AND FUEL IN GENERAL AND POST HOSPITALS.

A good *"range"* heated with coal is unquestionably the best means of cooking for a general hospital, where it is possible to obtain it. Where it is supplied, there is no reason why the best results as to the *cuisine* should not be attained.

One or more properly constructed cooking-stoves answer nearly the same purpose: they are somewhat inferior in convenience and economy, but, on the whole, an excellent substitute where a range cannot be had.

These cooking-stoves may be made to burn either wood or coal. They should be so constructed as to give ovens for baking as well as conveniences for boiling, and cooking over an open fire.

Whether ranges or stoves be employed, the cooking-utensils, such as caldrons for soup, coffee, baking-pans, &c., should be procured with them, to secure their being properly constructed, as to form and size, to suit the amount of fire in each case.

These utensils should be—large iron caldrons for boiling soup or meat, holding from ten to twenty gallons, large block-tin boilers for coffee and tea, with a faucet about two inches from the bottom, and holding about the same quantities, with stew-pans, gridirons, &c. &c.

Too much care cannot be exercised in the management of the fires. The success of the cooking is to a great extent dependent upon it. Thus, in the preparation of soups, a slow, moderate fire, steadily kept up, is indispensable; while for roasting or baking, a brisk, hot fire is equally necessary. The management of the several varieties of ranges and stoves is best acquired by practice and by steady endeavors to maintain the degree of heat necessary for the cooking actually going on. No general rules can, therefore, be laid down in the brief space of this volume, and much must depend in every case upon the discretion of the cook, over whom the steward must keep up a proper superintendence, never forgetting that, while the cooks are responsible to him, he is responsible to the surgeon, for the con dition of the kitchen and the quality of the cooking.

FUEL for the hospital, whether wood or coal, is to be obtained of the quartermaster, on a requisition signed by the surgeon and approved by the commanding officer.

The following form is that directed in regulations:—*

---

* Revised Reg., Quartermaster's Depart., Form No. 30, p. 208.

FORM OF REQUISITION FOR FUEL.

Requisition for Fuel for the Hospital at ———, *for the month of* ———, 186 .

	WOOD.			COAL.		REMARKS.
	Cord.	Feet.	Inches.	Bushels.	Pounds.	
						Number of fires.
Total...						

I certify, on honor, that the above requisition is correct and just, and that I have not drawn fuel for any part of the time above charged.

Surgeon U.S.A.

Received at ...., the .... of .... 186 , of ...., Assistant Quartermaster U.S.A., ... cords .... feet .... inches of wood and .... of coal, in full of the above requisition.

Surgeon U.S.A.

(Copies of this requisition should be kept on file by the Steward.)

Fuel is to be drawn monthly. It should be kept in a place appropriated to the purpose, convenient to the kitchen. If wood, it should be neatly piled after having been cut or sawed into lengths such as needed for use. If coal, it should be kept under cover, as it deteriorates from exposure.

SECTION III.—FIRES AND FUEL IN CAMP-HOSPITALS.

The best cooking apparatus in the camp-hospital is a good camp cooking-stove. Very frequently, however, this is not attainable. The hospital steward is then obliged to resort to other means, which are more or less imperfect. The plan generally resorted to is that usually employed by our soldiers in the field. It is very simple. A trench eighteen inches wide, and nine or ten deep, is cut of a length which varies in accordance with the amount of cooking to be done. A forked stake is driven into the ground at each end of the trench, and a pole laid across in the forks. From this pole the kettles for boiling soup, coffee, &c. are suspended. Pieces of meat for roasting may be suspended by strings. Pans for stewing are placed over the fire, supported upon properly placed stones, or, in locations where—as often happens in this country—these cannot be obtained, upon sods cut about twelve inches square, and properly piled on each side of the trench for this purpose.

The figure illustrates the plan.

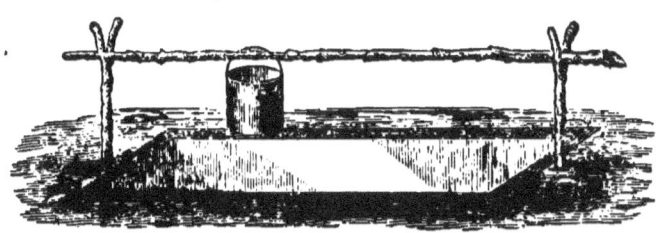

Where it is possible to line the trench with brick and build a chimney at one end, it will be found an improvement; but even then the plan is a very imperfect one. (See figure).

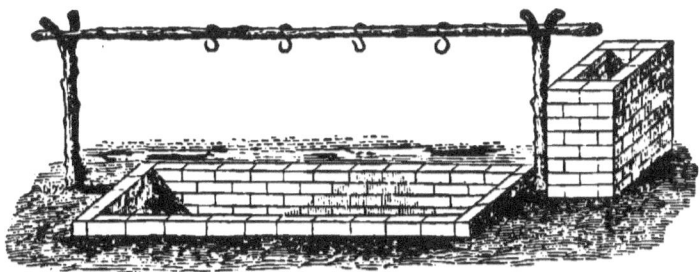

The objection to these plans is that changes in the direction of the wind interfere constantly with the steadiness of the fire.

To obviate this difficulty is the great practical question in building extemporaneous field-fires. The plan of the Turkish soldiers in the Russian war is commended by Miss Nightingale as attaining this end :*—

"The Turkish soldier cuts a trench, six inches deep and six wide, in a curve against a bank, natural or artifical, not less than two feet high. He cuts a few trenches of like size in the earth, radiating inward from the curvilinear trench : he places his kettles upon the intersection of these trenches, and the result is a steady draught leading upward against the bank; no blast of air blows through any one trench so as to disturb the fire."

I have never seen this plan tried; but it is simple, rational, and appears likely to attain the desired objects.

Another plan, and well adapted to a clayey soil, is that adopted by the salt-boilers of New York. A hole three feet square and two deep is dug in the slope of a hill. From this a shaft is run laterally about one foot square and six long: at the extreme end of this a shaft is sunk

---

* Notes on Matters Affecting the Health, Efficiency, and Hospital Administration of the British Army. By Florence Nightingale. London, 1858. Printed for private distribution; pp. 402.

vertically, and a chimney built: three holes, of such diameter that the camp-kettles will not sink through, are pierced at equal distances along the horizontal shaft. The fire is built in the square hole, the draught is borne through the lateral shaft to the chimney. The kettles for coffee, soup, &c. are set over the holes; the immediate fire may be used for roasting and boiling. (See figure on p. 218).

The accompanying illustrative diagram is from the little pamphlet by Capt. J. M. Sanderson, C. S. of volunteers, on "camp-fires and camp-cooking," which was recently distributed from the Commissary-General's office.

Lastly, very satisfactory cooking on a small scale may be done over fires arranged as described in the remarks on warming hospital tents.*

Fuel for camp-hospitals is either obtained, as in barracks, by requisition on the quartermaster, or by cutting wood in neighboring forests, or collecting it from whatever source may offer in individual cases. The duty of collecting it belongs to the police of

---

* See Part II. chap. ii. sect. iii.

Outside View.

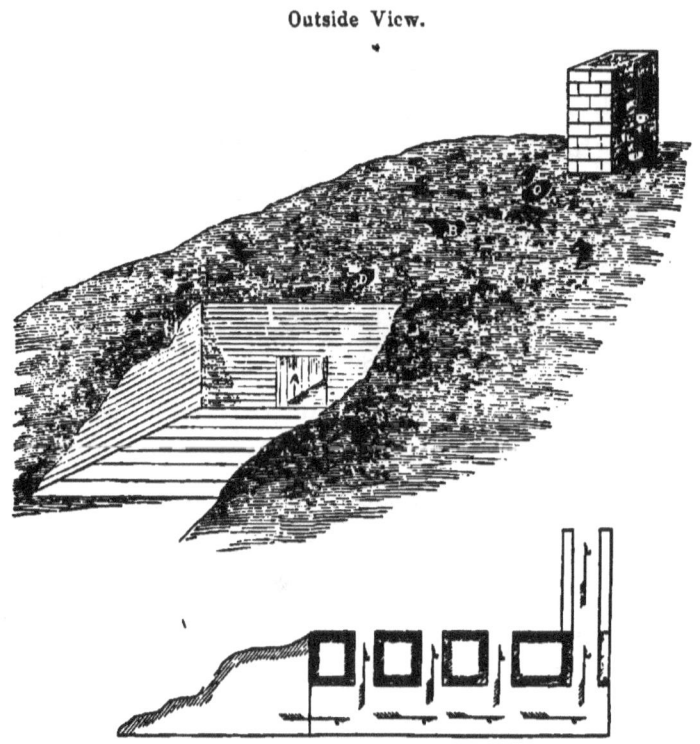

the regiment or brigade to which the hospital belongs, who, while collecting wood for the general cooking of the command, collects it also for the hospital. The order for this purpose is given by the commanding officer, at the request of the surgeon.

CHAPTER IV.

Cooking in Hospitals.

SECTION I.—GENERAL REMARKS.

PERHAPS no subject is more worthy of attention in a hospital than the quality of the food and the character of the cooking. In the latter there is certainly greater room for improvement in United States army hospitals than in the former. The rations furnished by the commissary department are generally of good quality and in good condition; the articles purchased with the hospital fund ought certainly to be of good quality; but, however good the raw articles may be, bad cooking will impair their nutritive value, as well as the relish with which they are eaten by the patients.

Cooking serves for two distinct purposes. In the first place, it serves so to modify the food by the heat employed as to cause it to be more readily dissolved during digestion. But in the second place, also, it serves, by rendering the food more palatable, to incite the digestive secretions, and thus not only to increase the appetite, but also the energy of digestion.

Now, on the one hand, the heat may be erroneously so employed as to have the effect rather of rendering articles of food insoluble, and therefore difficult of digestion, or of producing destructive changes, as where the food is more or less burned; and, on the other hand, the food may be so cooked as to be unpalatable, which will have the effect not merely of diminishing the appetite and causing the patient to eat less food than he should, but impairs directly his digestive energies, so that he does not digest what he does eat, as well as he would have done had it been properly prepared.

As an illustration of the erroneous management of heat, may be cited the preparation of soups, in which, if a brisk ebullition be kept up from the first, the exterior of the pieces of meat is rapidly hardened, and the full strength is never taken up into the soup as it is where the water put in cold is gradually brought nearly, but not quite, to the boiling-point, and allowed to simmer for several hours.

In other cases a hot fire is required, as in

roasting, where if the fire is brisk the outside of the piece rapidly becomes crisp, and all the juices are kept in, while if the fire is slow the juices leak gradually away, and the meat is left tasteless and insipid.

With the hope of contributing somewhat to the improvement of the cooking in the hospitals of the United States army, a number of receipts for ordinary and extra diet are here given. Most of these receipts are those of the celebrated M. Soyer, and have not only been thoroughly tested during the Crimean War, but have most of them received an approval, based upon actual experience, by United States army surgeons.

The use of these or similar receipts will insure the palatability and proper preparation of the food. As to its palatability, the steward may adopt a very simple rule. The food must be regarded as deficient in this respect unless it gives satisfaction to the patients. Of course, there are some grumblers who will find fault under all circumstances; but where the cooking is generally complained of, it must be bad, and the steward should at once consult with the cooks, and, if necessary, with the surgeon, as to the means of improving it.

SECTION II.—RECEIPTS ADAPTED TO THE ORDINARY DIET IN HOSPITALS.

No. 1. *Coffee for ten men.—(Soyer's method.)** —Put 9 pints of water into a canteen, saucepan (or other vessel) on the fire; when boiling, add 7½ oz. of coffee; mix them well together with a spoon or piece of wood; leave on the fire a few minutes longer, or until just beginning to boil. Take it off, and pour in 1 pint of cold water; let the whole remain ten minutes, or a little longer; the dregs will fall to the bottom, and the coffee will be clear. Pour it from one vessel into another, leaving the dregs at the bottom; add 2 teaspoonfuls of sugar to the pint. If milk is to be had, make 2 pints less of coffee, and add that much milk; boiled milk is preferable.

REMARKS.—This receipt, properly carried out, would give 10 pints of coffee, or 1 pint per man. The allowance of coffee in the army ration is 1 lb. to ten men.

---

* Most of the following receipts are taken, with little or no alteration, from "Soyer's Culinary Campaign." By Alexis Soyer. London, 1857.

This quantity would give 8 oz. to 10 pints of coffee for breakfast, and the same for supper, or a little more than M. Soyer's allowance. If tea is used for supper, only half the ration of coffee should be drawn, and tea drawn for the rest. To calculate the quantity of coffee to be drawn upon the provision return in a hospital where coffee is used for breakfast only, the following rule may be given. *Divide the number of patients and attendants allowed to use coffee by two:* the result is the number of rations of coffee required per day.

In great hospitals the coffee is usually made in large caldrons or boilers, holding each enough for fifty or one hundred men.

The following modified receipt may be used:—

No. 2. *Hospital receipt for coffee for fifty men, allowing 1 pint to each.—Ingredients needed.—* Water, 5 gallons, milk, 1¼ gallon, sugar, 3½ lbs. *Directions.*—Put into the boiler 35 pints of water (4 gallons and 3 pints); bring it to a boil. When boiling, add 2½ lbs. of coffee; stir well until ebullition has thoroughly recommenced, say for four or five minutes; then lift the boiler off the fire, and pour in 5 pints (2½ quarts) of *cold* water. Let it stand about ten minutes, when the coffee may be carefully poured or drawn off into the coffee-pots, leaving the dregs behind. To every two quarts drawn off add a pint of milk (boiled milk is best) and 3 oz. of sugar. A seven or eight gallon coffee-boiler answers very well for this purpose. If coffee for a hundred men is to be cooked in a single vessel, use double the quantity.

REMARKS.—Two points in these receipts are of practical importance. First, the coffee is not to be introduced until the water is boiling, nor is it to be boiled too long. If this is neglected, the aroma is destroyed, and the coffee is muddy and insipid. Secondly, the subsequent addition of cold water causes the dregs to subside more rapidly, and "*clears*" the coffee.

No. 3. *Tea for eighty men.*—(*M. Soyer's receipt.*)—Put 40 quarts of water in a boiler to boil; place the rations of tea in a fine net very loose, or in a large perforated ball; give one minute to boil; take out the fire, if too much; shut down the cover: in ten minutes it is ready for use.

No. 4. *Tea for fifty men.*—(*Hospital Receipt based on Soyer's Receipt.*)—*Ingredients needed.*— 20 quarts of water, 5 of milk, 6 oz. of tea, and 3¼ pounds of sugar. *Directions.*—Put into the boiler 20 quarts of water, 2½ gallons. Bring it to a boil. When boiling, introduce 6 oz. of tea tied up loosely in a bag of bobinet or mosquito netting, to prevent the leaves becoming diffused throughout the liquor. Allow it to boil one or two minutes; then lift the boiler off the fire, and allow it to stand on the stove or range, but not over the coals, for ten or fifteen minutes to draw. While drawing, the boiler should be covered. Stir in now 5 quarts of milk and 3¼ pounds of sugar, and the tea is ready for the table.

REMARKS.—The aim of this process is *not* to boil the tea, but to allow it to macerate (or draw) in boiling water.

No. 5. *Codfish Hash.*—Put the salt fish to soak over night in lukewarm water, fleshy side downward. Next morning put it in a pot with fresh water, and simmer till it is tender. Pick the flesh from the skin, rejecting the bones; chop it fine, and mix with three times its weight of boiled potatoes, moistening the mixture with pork scraps and *dip* (*i.e.* pork cut up fine and tried out). The addition of some milk will be found a great improvement. About 12 pounds of fish and 36 of potatoes prepared in this way will make a good breakfast relish for one hundred men.

No. 6. *Beef Soup for fifty men.—Soyer's Army Receipt.—Ingredients needed.*—Cold water, 7½ gals., fresh beef, 50 lbs., rice, 3 lbs., fresh vegetables (viz. carrots, onions, turnips, potatoes, parsley, &c. &c.), 8 lbs. (or desiccated vegetables, 1½ lbs.), 10 small tablespoonfuls of salt, 1 tablespoonful of pepper. *Directions.*—Put all the ingredients, except the rice, into the boiler; gradually bring it to a boil; then add the rice, and simmer three hours, when it will be ready to serve. Before serving, the fat should be skimmed off and kept in a clean vessel; it will serve as an excellent substitute for butter for many cooking purposes. The meat may be eaten with the soup, or, if other meat is given at dinner, may be kept for breakfast relishes.

REMARKS.—This soup, which is given by M. Soyer among his army receipts, is perhaps inferior, on the whole, to the next receipt.

No. 7. *Semi-stewed Beef and Soup for one hundred men.*—(*Soyer's Hospital Receipt.*)—*Ingredients needed.*—Cold water, 130 pints (16¼ gallons), fresh beef, 70 lbs. (in pieces of 4 or 5 lbs.), mixed fresh vegetables, 12 lbs. (carrots, onions, parsley, turnips, potatoes, &c., according to taste or convenience), barley, or rice, 9 lbs. 6 oz., salt, 1 lb. 7 oz., flour 1 lb. 4 oz., sugar, 1 lb. 4 oz., pepper, 1 oz. *Directions.*—Put all the ingredients into the caldron at once, except the flour; set it on the fire, and, when beginning to boil, diminish the heat and simmer gently for two hours and a half; then add to the soup the flour, which has been first mixed with enough water to form a light batter; stir well together with a large spoon; boil another half-hour; skim off the fat; take out the meat, and serve the soup and meat separate. The soup should be stirred now and then while making, to prevent burning, or sticking to the sides of the caldron.

REMARKS.—The joints are cooked whole, and afterwards cut up into equal portions, one for each man. The meat cooked in this way is more nutritious. Where fresh vegetables cannot be obtained, 3 lbs. of mixed desiccated vegetables may be substituted for 12 of fresh.

Variations.—The addition of a quarter of a pound of curry powder, or of half a pint of burnt-sugar water, gives an agreeable diversity in appearance and flavor.

No. 8. *Semi-stewed Mutton and Soup for one hundred men.*—(*Soyer's Hospital Receipt.*)—*Ingredients.*—The same as in the last receipt, except that mutton is substituted for beef.

Proceed the same as for beef, except that, as mutton needs less cooking than beef, the joints should be taken out before the flour is added, and kept warm in a suitable pan till time for serving.

No. 9. *Plain Irish Stew for fifty men.*— (*Soyer's Receipt.*)—*Ingredients.*—Fresh mutton or beef, 50 lbs., large onions, 8 lbs., whole potatoes, 12 lbs., 8 tablespoonfuls of salt, 3 tablespoonfuls of pepper; water, a sufficient quantity. *Directions.*—Cut the meat into pieces of a quarter of a pound each; put the ingredients into the pan with enough water to cover them all. Set it on the fire, and keep up gentle ebullition, stirring occasionally. for an hour and a half for mutton, and two hours for beef. Then mash some of the potatoes to thicken the gravy, and serve.

Variations.—Fresh veal, or pork, may be used instead, when convenient.

No. 10. "*Soyer's Food*" *for fifty men.*—*Ingredients.*—Fresh beef, 50 lbs., onions, 7 lbs., flour, 1½ lbs., 10 tablespoonfuls of salt, 2 tablespoonfuls of pepper, 4 tablespoonfuls of sugar, water, 18 quarts. *Directions.*—Cut the beef into pieces of a quarter of a pound each, slice the onions, and introduce all the solid ingredients except the flour, with a little of the water, into the boiler. Set it on the fire and let it stew, stirring occasionally, for twenty to thirty minutes, or till it forms a thick gravy; then add a pound and a half of flour; mix well together, and add the rest of the water; stir well for a minute or two; regulate the stove to a moderate heat, and let simmer for about two hours.

Variations.—A pound of rice may be added to great advantage, also plain dumplings, and potatoes, or mixed vegetables.

No. 11. *Suet Dumplings for Soups or Stews.*—(*Soyer's Receipt.*)—*Ingredients.*—Half a pound of flour, half a teaspoonful of salt, a quarter of a pound of chopped fat pork (or of beef suet), and eight tablespoonfuls of water, with two onions chopped fine, if convenient. *Directions.*—Mix well into a thick paste; divide into pieces of convenient size; roll them in flour and put into the soup, or stew, about half an hour before it is done.

REMARKS.—A few dumplings made in this manner, and scattered through the soup, are a great addition, but they should not be too abundant.

No. 12. *To boil Salt Beef (or Pork) for fifty men.—(Soyer's Receipt.)*—Put 50 lbs. of meat in pieces of 3 or 4 lbs. each into a boiler; fill the boiler with water, and let the meat soak all night. Next morning wash the meat well, and pour away the salt water. Fill the boiler with fresh water; boil gently three hours, and serve. Skim off the fat, which, when cold, is an excellent substitute for butter.

For salt pork, proceed as above, or boil half beef and half pork. The pieces of beef should be smaller than those of pork, as beef requires longer to cook. Where salt meat cannot be soaked all night, it should be parboiled for twenty minutes, and then the water poured off, fresh poured on, and the cooking commenced.

No. 13. *Soup from the Liquor in which Salt Pork has been boiled.*—The liquor in which salt pork has been boiled can be made into a very good soup with peas, or beans. Add to the liquor in which 50 lbs. of salt pork has been cooked 5 lbs. split peas, ½ lb. brown sugar, 2 tablespoonfuls of pepper, and 10 onions; simmer gently till the peas are reduced to a pulp, and serve. Broken biscuit may be introduced. This will make an excellent mess. Beans properly soaked may be substituted for the peas.

No. 14.—*Stewed Salt Beef and Pork for one hundred men.*—*Ingredients.*—Well-soaked beef, 30 lbs. cut into pieces of ¼ lb. each, pork, 20 lbs., sugar, 1½ lbs., onions, sliced, 8 lbs. water, 25 quarts, rice, 4 lbs. *Directions.*—Introduce all the ingredients into a boiler; simmer gently for three hours; skim the fat off the top, and serve.

REMARKS.—The beef and pork must be well soaked over night, according to the directions given in Receipt No. 12.

No. 15. *Bean soup for one hundred men.* *Ingredients.*—8 quarts of beans, 30 lbs. of pork, half a dozen onions, salt, ½ lb., pepper, 1 oz., water, 120 pints (15 gallons). *Directions.*— Soak the beans over night in cold water. Cut the pork into pieces of from three to five pounds each.

At eight o'clock in the morning the beans are to be put into a caldron filled with water, and boiled for two hours and a half, when the water is to be poured off and the beans are to be added to the pork-liquor next to be described. The pork is to be introduced into another caldron, at quarter-past eight o'clock, and boiled briskly for an hour, when the liquid is to be poured off and replaced by clean *hot* water, 120 pints to 30 lbs. of pork. The pork is now to be boiled an hour and a half longer, when it is to be taken out and laid aside to be served separately. The beans are then added to the liquid in which the pork was boiled, with the salt, pepper, and the onions (chopped or sliced). After fifteen minutes' more boiling, the beans are to be mashed with a wooden spoon made for the purpose, and the soup, which is now ready, is to be served with a slice of pork in a separate dish.

No. 16. *Bean Soup for one hundred men.*
—(*American Army Receipt.*)—*Ingredients.*—8 quarts of beans, 20 lbs. of pork, half a dozen onions, salt, ½ lb., pepper, 1 oz., water, 120 pints (15 gallons). *Directions.*—Soak the beans over night. Early in the morning put them into a caldron with the salt and water, and boil steadily for three hours, or until the beans are so well done that they can be strained through a sieve, leaving their skins on the sieve. They are then to be so strained, after which the pork, cut in slices, the onions, chopped fine, and the pepper, are to be added, and the boiling continued two to three hours longer, or till the pork is done tender, when the soup is ready.

In making this soup, good soft water is required. At posts where the water is hard, rain-water must be substituted. The caldron must be clean and free from grease, and grease in every shape must be avoided until the beans are *done.*

No. 17. *Browning for Soups.*—Put ½ lb. of moist sugar into an iron pan, and melt it over a moderate fire, stirring it continually till quite black, which will take about twenty-five minutes; it must color by degrees, as too sudden a heat will make it bitter: then add 2 quarts of water, and in ten minutes the sugar will be dissolved. You may then bottle it for use. It will keep good for a month, and will always be found very useful.

No. 18. *Baked Pork and Beans.*—The beans and pork, having been soaked over night, are boiled separately in the morning for about two hours. The pork is then put into pans, surrounded and covered by the beans, a little pepper added, and baked one hour by a moderate fire.

No. 19. *Corned Beef and Cabbage.*—The beef, having been soaked in fresh water over night, is placed in a caldron and simmered over a moderate fire for two hours and a half, skimming carefully every fifteen or twenty minutes. As much cabbage as the water will cover is then introduced, and the ebullition is to be continued gently for an hour and a half.

No. 20. *Boiled Potatoes.*—Wash the potatoes, and put them with their skins on into the caldron: throw in a handful of salt, and fill the vessel with cold water. Put it on the fire, and bring it to a boil. When the water boils, throw in a little cold water to check it: do so two or three times. When the potatoes are very nearly cooked, pour off all the water, and stand the kettle over the fire till the steam evaporates. This process will make the potatoes mealy.

No. 21. *Indian Mush for one hundred men.*—(*American Army Receipt.*)—*Ingredients.*—Indian meal, 20 lbs., water, 70 pints (8¾ gallons), salt, 6 oz. Moisten slightly the meal with water. It will require about one gallon and three-fourths for this purpose. Have the rest of the water—say 7 gallons—in the caldron boiling; add the salt, then stir in the moistened meal. The stirring should be continued after all the meal is in, to prevent burning. From twenty minutes to half an hour will be found long enough to boil. The above quantities will make 100 pints of mush, or a little more. One pint may be served to each man, with molasses or milk. If milk, one pint should be allowed to each patient; if molasses, one gallon to one hundred men.

REMARKS.—If the meal is stirred in *dry*, the mush will be lumpy.

No. 22. *Plain Boiled Rice.*—(*Soyer's Receipt.*) —Rice, ½ lb., water, 2 quarts, salt, 1 teaspoonful, or in that proportion for larger quantities. Put the salt and water into the stew-pan or boiler. When boiling, add the rice, previously well washed. Boil for ten minutes, or till each grain becomes rather soft. Drain it on a colander. Slightly grease the pot with butter; put the rice back into it; let it swell slowly for about twenty minutes near the fire or in a slow oven; each grain will then swell up and be well separated. It is then ready for use.

No. 23. *Bread.*

When the hospital is not situated near a Government bakery, it is desirable for it to be able to bake its own bread. For this purpose the "Shiraz oven" may be obtained by requisition on the Chief of the Commissariat. One of these ovens will be found ample to do the baking for about three hundred patients. The following receipts are copied from the little pamphlet on Camp Fires and Camp Cookery, by Captain J. M. Sanderson, C. S. of Volunteers.[*]

---

[*] Camp Fires and Camp Cookery; or, Culinary Hints for the

"*To make Yeast.*—Fill a kettle three-fourths full of clean, clear water; place it over a brisk fire, and, when it boils, add three good handfuls of hops; then put into the yeast-tub four pounds of flour, and strain into it, from the kettle, enough of the hot "hop-water" to make a paste, working it until it is perfectly free from lumps. By this time the hops in the kettle will be sufficiently boiled, and must be strained into the yeast-tub, and stirred with a wooden paddle until thoroughly amalgamated. Let it stand until it cools a little,—about blood-heat,—and add three pints of cracked malt and two quarts of stock yeast, mixing it all well together to prevent any lumps remaining, and setting it away in some quiet, warm place, where it will remain undisturbed, for fifteen hours; then it must be strained before using. Care must be taken *always* to keep enough on hand for stock for the next making.

"*To make Bread.*—The first process is to pre-

Soldiers, including Receipts for making Bread in "the Portable Field Oven" furnished by the Subsistence Department. By Captain J. M. Sanderson, C.S. of Volunteers. Published for distribution to the troops, Head-Quarters "Army of the Potomac," January, 1862.

pare the *ferment*. This is formed by boiling thoroughly a peck and a half of potatoes, with their skins on, which you place in a barrel kept exclusively for that purpose, adding six pounds of flour, and mashing them well together. This is called "scalding the flour." Then add cold water until it is cool enough to enable you to put your hands in, and break up the potatoes as fine as possible, so as to obtain all their virtue. Then add about six pailfuls of warm water, and six quarts of yeast. Stir it well together, and place it in a warm spot, where it will not be disturbed. Two good-sized tubs, made of salt or sugar barrels, would be the best receptacle for it, as it requires space to work in. This should be made at night, and will be ready for use in the morning after it is carefully strained.

"The second process is making the dough. This is done by sifting into the trough a barrel and a half of flour, one-third of which is pinned or blocked up at one end by the "pin-board" or wooden slide. To this you add three and a half pounds of salt and three and a half pailfuls of "ferment," with four pailfuls of hot water,—not so hot, however, as to scald your ferment (in summer, cold water is used instead of hot),—and mix well together, kneading thoroughly and faithfully, adding to it gradually all the flour in the trough until it is of one consistency. It must then be placed at one end of the trough, and again pinned in by the slide, leaving space enough, however, to allow it to prove. To effect this requires at least two hours, when it will be ready to "work off," which is done by "throwing" it out of the trough, in masses, on to the table or cover on the other side of the room or tent. It is then cut into pieces and weighed, or "scaled off," and immediately moulded into shapes or loaves. This requires one man to scale, one to form into loaves, and a third to "pan it away," where it remains for at least forty minutes before placing it in the oven. In the mean time the ovens are heated, the coals and ashes drawn out, and the interior thoroughly swabbed out, top and bottom. If too hot, wet the swab and dampen the oven. The pans containing the dough are then set in, by means of the heel or wooden spade, the doors closed, and the hot coals and ashes placed against them, in order to heat all sides equally. Fifty minutes is the time generally required to bake the usual-sized army loaves; if larger, a longer period will be required.

"The amount of ferment made in accordance with this receipt will be sufficient for three batches of 288 loaves each. The first batch will require four hours in preparing and baking; the second and third, two hours each.

"Potatoes, hops, and malt should always be kept on hand, and a portion of the yeast invariably retained as stock. To commence with, it will be necessary to obtain brewer's yeast; but after making the first essay you can always be independent."

SECTION III.—RECEIPTS FOR EXTRA DIETS.

(*Soyer's Receipts.*)

No. 1. *Beef Tea. Receipt for 6 pints.*—Cut 3 lbs. of beef into pieces the size of walnuts, and chop up the bones, if any; put it into a convenient-sized kettle with ½ lb. of mixed vegetables, such as onions, leeks, celery, turnips, carrots (or one or two of these, if all cannot be obtained), 1 oz. of salt, a little pepper, 1 teaspoonful of sugar, 2 oz. of butter, and ½ pint of water. Set it on a sharp fire for ten minutes or a quarter of an hour, stirring now and then with a spoon, till it forms a rather thick gravy at bottom, but not brown; then add 7 pints of hot or cold water,—but hot is preferable. When boiling, let it simmer gently for an hour; skim off all the fat, strain it through a sieve, and serve.

No. 2. *Thick Beef Tea.*—Dissolve a large teaspoonful of arrow-root in a gill of water, and pour it into the beef tea above described twenty minutes before passing through the sieve.

No. 3. *Beef Tea with Calves'-foot Jelly or Isinglass.*—Add ¼ oz. calves'-foot gelatine or isinglass to the above quantity of beef tea, when cooking, previous to serving.

No. 4. *Mutton and Veal Tea.*—Mutton and veal will make good tea by proceeding precisely the same as above. The addition of a small quantity of aromatic herbs is always desirable. If no fresh vegetables are at hand, use 2 oz. of mixed preserved vegetables to any of the above receipts.

No. 5. *Chicken Broth.*—Put in a stew-pan a fowl, 3 pints of water, 2 teaspoonfuls of rice, 1 teaspoonful of salt, a middle-sized onion, or

2 oz. of mixed vegetables; boil the whole gently for three-quarters of an hour: if an old fowl, simmer from one hour and a half to two hours, adding 1 pint more water; skim off the fat, and serve.

NOTE.—A light mutton broth may be made precisely the same, by using a pound and a half of scrag of mutton instead of fowl.

No. 6. *Beef Essence.*—Cut 1 pound of lean but tender beef into small dice, and introduce them into a bottle, which is to be corked and stood in a pot of water; boil for three hours; then strain off the liquor by putting the meat, after all that can be is poured off, in a linen bag and expressing. A little pepper and salt may be added.

No. 7. *Sweet Rice.*—Add to ½ lb. of rice plain boiled, as directed in Receipt No. 22, p. 236, 1 oz. of butter, 2 tablespoonfuls of sugar, a little cinnamon, a quarter of a pint of milk; stir it with a fork, and serve. A little currant jelly or jam may be added to the rice.

No. 8. *Rice with Gravy.*—Add to the same

quantity of rice 4 tablespoonfuls of the essence of beef, a little fresh butter, half a teaspoonful of salt; stir together with a fork, and serve.

No. 9. *Plain Oatmeal.*—Put in a pan ¼ lb. of oatmeal, 1½ oz. of sugar, half a teaspoonful of salt, and 3 pints of water; boil slowly for twenty minutes, stirring continually, and serve. A quarter of a pint of boiled milk, an ounce of butter, and a little pounded cinnamon or spice, added previous to serving, is a good variation.

No. 10. *Calves'-Foot Jelly.*—Put in a proper-sized stew-pan 2¼ oz. of calves'-foot gelatine, 4 oz. of white sugar, 4 whites of eggs and shells, the peel of a lemon, the juice of 3 middle-sized lemons, half a pint of marsala or sherry wine. Beat all well together with the egg-beater for a few minutes; then add 4½ pints of cold water; set it on a slow fire, and keep whipping it till boiling. Set it on the corner of the stove, partly covered with the lid, upon which you place a few pieces of burning charcoal; let it simmer gently for ten minutes, and strain it through a jelly-bag. It is then ready to be put in ice or some cool place.

For orange jelly, use only 1 lemon and 2

oranges. Any delicate flavor may be introduced.

No. 11. *Farina Pudding.*—Boil 3 pints of milk, into which, while boiling, sprinkle slowly one-quarter of a pound of farina (Hecker's farina). Continue the boiling three-quarters of an hour. Turn it into a jelly-mould, and place it on ice or in cold water to stiffen. It may be eaten with pulverized sugar.

The boiling should be conducted in a double boiler, or in a saucepan set into a pan of water to boil in such a way that the bottom of the saucepan does not touch the bottom of the pan: this is to avoid burning.

No. 12. *Corn Starch Blanc-Mange.*—Beat 6 tablespoonfuls of corn starch (Duryea's Maizena) thoroughly with 3 eggs; add to it 1 quart of milk nearly boiling, and previously salted a little: allow it to boil a few minutes, stirring briskly. Flavor with lemon or vanilla, and pour into a mould to stiffen. It may be sweetened before cooking, or may be cooked without sweetening, and eaten with pulverized sugar or a sauce.

No. 13. *Boiled Custard* (*Corn Starch*).—
Heat 1 quart of milk nearly to boiling; add
2 tablespoonfuls of corn starch previously
mixed with a little milk, 3 eggs well beaten,
with 4 tablespoonfuls of powdered sugar, half
a teaspoonful of salt, and a small piece of butter.
Flavor with lemon or vanilla. Let it boil up
once or twice, stirring briskly, and it is done.
To be eaten cold.

No. 14. *Calves'-Foot Jelly, from Calves' Feet.*—
This jelly requires to be made the day previous
to being used, requiring to be very hard to
extract the fat.

Take 2 calves' feet, cut them up, and boil in 3
quarts of water; as soon as it boils, remove it
to the corner of the fire and simmer for five
hours, keeping it skimmed; pass through a hair
sieve into a basin, and let it remain until quite
hard; then remove the oil and fat, and wipe
the top dry. Place in a stew-pan ½ pint of
water, 1 pint of sherry, ½ lb. of lump sugar,
the juice of 4 lemons, the rinds of 2, and the
whites and shells of 5 eggs; whisk until the
sugar is melted; then add the jelly, place it on
the fire, and whisk until boiling; pass it through
a jelly-bag, pouring that back again which

comes through first, until quite clear: it is then ready for use. Vary the flavor according to fancy.

Ox-feet or cow-heel may be used instead of calves' feet, where these cannot be had; but they require an hour more simmering. In summer, ice must be used to set the jelly.

No. 15. *Sago Jelly.*—Put into a pan 3 oz. of sago, 1½ oz. of sugar, half a lemon-peel cut very thin, ¼ teaspoonful of ground cinnamon, or a small stick of the same; put to it 3 pints of water and a little salt; boil ten minutes, or a little longer, stirring continually, until rather thick; then add a little port, sherry, or marsala wine: mix well, and serve hot or cold.

No. 16. *Arrow-Root Milk.*—Put into a pan 4 oz. of arrow-root, 3 oz. of sugar, the peel of half a lemon, ¼ teaspoonful of salt, 2½ pints of milk; set it on the fire, stir round gently, boil for ten minutes, and serve. If no lemons are at hand, a little essence of any kind will do.

When short of milk, use half water: half an ounce of fresh butter is an improvement before serving.

No. 17. *Thick Arrow-Root Panada.*—Put in a pan 5 oz. of arrow-root, 2½ oz. of white sugar, the peel of half a lemon, ¼ teaspoonful of salt, 4 pints of water; mix all well, set on the fire, boil for ten minutes: it is then ready. Milk is preferable to water if at hand.

No. 18. *Arrow-Root Water.*—Put into a pan 3 oz. of arrow-root, 2 oz. of white sugar, the peel of a lemon, ¼ teaspoonful of salt, 4 pints of water; mix well, set on the fire, boil for ten minutes: it is then ready to serve, either hot or cold.

No. 19. *Rice Water.*—Put 7 pints of water to boil; add to it 2 oz. of rice well washed, 2 oz. of sugar, the peel of two-thirds of a lemon; boil gently for three-quarters of an hour; it will reduce to 5 pints: strain through a colander: it is then ready.

No. 20. *Barley Water.*—Put into a saucepan 7 pints of water, 2 oz. of barley, which stir now and then while boiling; add 2 oz. of white sugar, and the rind of half a lemon thinly peeled; let it boil gently for about two hours, without covering it: pass it through a sieve or colander:

it is then ready. The barley and lemon may be left in it.

No. 21. *Soyer's Plain Lemonade.*—Thinly peel the third part of a lemon, which put in a bowl with 2 tablespoonfuls of sugar; roll the lemon in your hand upon the table to soften it, cut it into two lengthwise, squeeze the juice over the peel, &c., stir round for a minute with a spoon to form a sort of syrup; pour over a pint of water, mix well, and remove the pips: it is then ready for use.

If a very large lemon, fresh and full of juice, you may make a pint and a half, to a quart, adding sugar and peel in proportion to the increase of water. The juice only of the lemon and sugar will make lemonade, but will then be deprived of the aroma which the rind contains.

No. 22. *Semi-Citric Lemonade.*—*Receipt for 50 Pints.*—Put 1 oz. of citric acid to dissolve in a pint of water; peel 20 lemons thinly, and put the peel in a large vessel with 3 lbs. 2 oz. of white sugar well broken; roll each lemon on the table to soften it, which will facilitate the extraction of the juice; cut them into two, and press out the juice into a colander or sieve over the peel and sugar; then pour half a pint of water through the colander, so as to leave no juice remaining; triturate the sugar, juice, and peel together for a minute or two with a spoon, so as to form a sort of syrup and extract the aroma from the peel; add the dissolved citric acid, mix all well together, pour on 50 pints of cold water, stir all well together: it is then ready A little ice in summer is a great addition.

No. 23. *Soyer's Cheap Crimean Lemonade.*— Put into a bowl 2 tablespoonfuls of sugar, ½ tablespoonful of lime-juice; mix well for one minute; add 1 pint of water, and the beverage is ready. A little rum is an agreeable addition.

No. 24. *Tartaric Lemonade.*—Dissolve 1 oz. of crystallized tartaric acid in a pint of cold water, which put in a large vessel: when dissolved, add 1 lb. 9 oz. of white or brown sugar (the former is preferable); mix well to form a thick syrup; add to it 24 pints of cold water, slowly mixing well: it is then ready.

A similar beverage may be made of citric acid, using, however, only 20 pints of water to each ounce.

No. 25. *Cheap Plain Rice Pudding without eggs or milk.*—Put on the fire, in a moderate-sized saucepan, 12 pints of water: when boiling, add to it 1 lb. of rice, 4 oz. of brown sugar, 1 large teaspoonful of salt, and the rind of a lemon thinly peeled; boil gently for half an hour, then strain all the water from the rice; add to the rice 3 oz. of sugar, 4 tablespoonfuls of flour, ½ teaspoonful of pounded cinnamon; stir it on the fire carefully for five or ten minutes; put it in a tin or a pie-dish, and bake.

The rice water poured off, as above directed, may be made into a beverage, the juice of a lemon being introduced to give it flavor.

No. 26. *Rich Rice Pudding.*—Put ½ lb. of washed rice in a stew-pan, 3 pints of milk, 1 pint of water, 3 oz. of sugar, 1 lemon-peel, 1 oz. of fresh butter; boil gently half an hour, or until the rice is tender; add 4 eggs well beaten, mix well, bake quickly for half an hour, and serve.

No. 27. *Boiled Rice Semi-Curried* (suitable for cases of commencing diarrhœa).—Put 1 quart of water in a pot or saucepan; when boiling, add ½ lb. of well-washed rice; boil fast for ten minutes; then drain the rice on a colander, put it in a saucepan greased slightly with butter, let it swell slowly near the fire, or in a slow oven, till tender; each grain will then be light and well separated; add a quarter of a teaspoonful of curry-powder, mix together lightly with a fork, and serve.

No. 28. *Batter Pudding.*—Break 2 fresh eggs in a basin, beat them well; add one tablespoonful and a half of flour, which beat up with your eggs with a fork until no lumps remain; add a gill of milk and a teaspoonful of salt; butter a bowl, pour in the mixture, put some water in a stew-pan, enough to immerge half-way up the cup or bowl: boil for twenty minutes, or till the pudding is well set; pass a knife to loosen it, turn out on a plate, pour pounded sugar over it, with or without a little butter, and serve.

No. 29. *Bread-and-Butter Pudding.*—Butter a tart-dish well, and sprinkle some currants all round it; then lay in a few slices of bread-and-butter; boil 1 pint of milk, pour it on 2 eggs well whipped, and then on the bread-and-butter: bake in a hot oven for half an hour. The currants may be omitted when not convenient.

No. 30. *Bread Pudding.*—Boil 1 pint of milk, with a piece of cinnamon and lemon-peel; pour it on 2 oz. of bread-crumbs, then add 2 eggs, ½ oz. of currants, and a little sugar: steam it in a buttered mould, or pan, for one hour.

No. 31. *Custard Pudding.*—Boil 1 pint of milk with a small piece of lemon-peel and half a bay-leaf for three minutes; then pour these on to 3 eggs; mix it with 1 oz. of sugar well together, and pour it into a buttered mould or pan: set this in a stew-pan with some water, steam it for twenty-five minutes, turn it out on a plate, and serve.

No. 32. *Stewed Macaroni.*—Put in a stew-pan 2 quarts of water, half a tablespoonful of salt, 2 oz. of butter; set on the fire; when boiling, add 1 lb. of macaroni, broken up rather small; when boiled very soft, throw off the water; mix well into the macaroni a tablespoonful of flour, add enough milk to make it of the consistency of melted butter, boil gently twenty minutes, add in a tablespoonful of either brown or white sugar, or honey, and serve.

A little cinnamon, nutmeg, lemon-peel, or orange-flower water may be introduced to impart a flavor; stir quick. A gill of milk or cream may be thrown in three minutes before serving. Nothing can be more light and nutritious than macaroni done in this way.

No. 33. *Macaroni Pudding.*—Put 2 pints of water to boil; add, when boiling, 2 oz. of macaroni, broken in small pieces; boil till tender; draw off the water, and add half a tablespoonful of flour, 2 oz. of white sugar, a quarter of a pint of milk, and boil together for ten minutes; beat an egg up, add it to the other ingredients with a nut of butter: mix well, and bake, or steam. It can be served plain, and may be flavored with either cinnamon, lemon, or some essence.

No. 34. *Sago Pudding.*—Put in a pan 4 oz. of sago, 2 oz. of sugar, half a lemon-peel, or a little cinnamon, a small nut of fresh butter, and half a pint of milk; boil for a few minutes, or until rather thick, stirring all the while. Beat up 2 eggs, and mix quickly with the same: it is then ready for either baking or steaming.

No. 35. *Tapioca Pudding.*—Put in a pan 2 oz. of tapioca, 1½ pint of milk, 1 oz. of white or brown sugar, and a little salt; set on the fire; boil gently for fifteen minutes, or until the tapioca is tender, stirring now and then to prevent its sticking to the bottom, or burning; then add 2 eggs well beaten : steam, or bake, and serve. It will take about twenty minutes steaming, or a quarter of an hour baking slightly. Flavor with either lemon, cinnamon, or any other essence.

No. 36. *Toast and Water.*—Cut a piece of crusty bread, about ¼ lb. in weight, place it upon a toasting-fork, and hold it about six inches from the fire; turn it often, and keep moving it gently until of a light yellow color; then place it nearer the fire, and when of a good brown chocolate color, put it in a jug and pour over 3 pints of boiling water; cover the jug until cold, then strain it into a clean vessel, and it is ready for use. Never leave the toast in it, for in summer it would cause fermentation in a short time.

A piece of apple, slowly toasted till it gets quite black, and added to the above, makes a very nice and refreshing drink for invalids.

No. 37.—*Figs and Apple Beverage.*—Have 2 quarts of water boiling, into which throw 6 dry figs previously opened, and 2 apples, cut into six or eight slices each; let the whole boil together twenty minutes, then pour them into a basin to cool: pass through a sieve. The figs, if drained, will be good to eat with a little sugar, or jam.

No. 38.—*Egg Soup.*—Beat an egg perfectly light, beating white and yolk at first separately, and when light mixing them well together; add a teaspoonful of powdered sugar, a little nutmeg, and while stirring briskly pour in a wineglassful of boiling water, and then add a wineglassful of sherry wine.

No. 39. *Omelets with Fine Herbs.* — Six eggs will make a nice omelet for two persons. Break them carefully into a bowl, as a tainted egg will spoil all the rest; add three-quarters of a tablespoonful of salt, a quarter ditto of pepper, two of chopped parsley, and half a one of fine-chopped onions. Beat them well. Put 2 oz. of butter in a clean frying-pan, place it on the fire, and, when the butter is very hot, pour in the eggs, which keep mixing quick with a spoon until all is delicately set; then let it slip to the edge of the pan *en masse*, laying hold of the handle and raising it slantwise, which will give an elongated form to the omelet; turning the edges, let it set a minute: turn on a dish, and serve.

No. 40. *For Bacon or Ham Omelets.*—Cut 2 oz. of ham or bacon, not too salt, in small dice; fry two or three minutes in the butter before putting in the eggs, and proceed as above.

No. 41. *Boiled Eggs.*—The water should be boiling before the eggs are introduced. Three minutes is long enough for soft-boiled and five for hard-boiled eggs.

No. 42. *Fried Steaks.*—Cut the steak in pieces of 8 oz. each; flatten them to the thickness of three-quarters of an inch, taking care that each piece contains a little fat. Put a clean frying-pan on the fire, with half an ounce of butter, which when browned a little is ready to receive the steak; keep it on a rather quick fire, turning it several times, and, when cooking, season each side with one-fourth of a teaspoonful of salt and a pinch of pepper. Six minutes will do the steak; and by pressing it with a fork or the finger you can ascertain if it is equally done through. When done, suspend the steak over the pan, to allow the melted fat, if any, which clings to the meat, to fall back into the pan.

No. 43. *Fried Chops.*—Have a fine chop weighing 8 oz., and three-quarters of an inch in thickness, without too much bone or fat. Cook the same as the steak, turning two or three times until well browned on either side. The fire for both should be brisk, as the surface of the meat becomes thereby carbonized and retains the juice.

No. 44. *Broiled Chops and Steaks.*—To broil either, place them on a gridiron over a sharp fire, and turn two or three times while cooking. Six minutes will do either. Season as for fried steaks.

More is lost in weight by broiling than by frying; but the flavor is better, and the meat is more succulent.

No. 45. *Roast and Grilled Fowls.*—Fowls should be roasted whole, and divided into diets according to size.

They should also be grilled whole, being divided up the back and trussed as usual for grilling. Rub over a little butter, and grill on a *moderate* fire, turning several times and keeping a light yellow color. When partly done, season with a small teaspoonful of salt and a little pepper. When done, rub over a little fresh butter: serve whole or in portions.

No. 46. *Fried Fish.*—Any kind of fish, though fried in fat, when properly done, does not retain the slightest particle of fat which would be prejudicial to the patient. This is avoided by having the fat at a proper degree of heat, which can be ascertained when it begins to smoke, and when all boiling has ceased. If you then dip your finger in water and let a drop fall into the fat, it will hiss loudly, if properly heated. Fat over-heated is equally unfit for use, which fact can be ascertained by the quantity of black smoke emitted by the fat, and by its making a disagreeable smell.

You may always ascertain when fish is done, as then the flesh separates from the bone easily with the aid of a fork, if tried in the thickest part. Take care that it does not over-do, which takes all the nutriment from the fish.

No. 47. *Broiled Fish.*—Trim as for frying, and dip in flour; butter very lightly over; put on a gridiron, previously well greased, to prevent sticking, over a very slow fire; turn once. Eight to ten minutes will do a fish of as many ounces' weight.

NOTE.—This is the lightest and the most difficult way in which fish can be dressed.

PART IV.

THE DISPENSARY.

CHAPTER I.

General Arrangement and Management of the Dispensary.

SECTION I.—REQUISITIONS FOR MEDICAL SUPPLIES.

REQUISITIONS for medical supplies are made out in duplicate by the senior medical officer of each hospital, post, or command. "If the supplies are to be obtained from the principal purveying depots, the requisitions will be made upon the Surgeon-General, on the 31st day of December annually; if from departments or field-depots, they will be made upon the medical director, at such times and for such periods as he may direct."*

Although these general rules are laid down, however, it is to be understood that many circumstances may exhaust the supplies sooner than was contemplated at the time of making the requisition; and, as no medical officer will

---

* Revised Reg., Art. XLIV. ₴ 1231.

be held blameless who permits his supplies to become exhausted without providing for replenishing them, it may become necessary at any time to make a special requisition to supply deficiencies.

"In every case of special requisition, a duplicate of the requisition shall at the same time be transmitted to the Surgeon-General, for his information, giving the name and station of the officer upon whom it is made."*

The following is the form of a requisition for medical supplies:—

---

* Revised Reg., Art. XLIV. § 1235.

Requisition for Medical and Hospital Supplies.

Command.—Officers, ...   Station, ...   Period, ...
Enlisted men, ...   All others entitled to medicines, ...   Total, ...

Articles, and Characters or Quantities.	On hand.	Wanted.	Articles, and Characters or Quantities.	On hand.	Wanted.
Acaciæ ....lb.					
Acidi acetici ....lb.					
" arseniosi ....oz.					
&c. &c.			&c. &c.		

Date ————.

———— ————, *Surgeon U.S.A.*

N.B.—Requisitions will exhibit the quantity of each and every article "on hand," whether more be wanted or not. They will be transmitted in duplicate, and by different mails.

On frontier and other posts remote from a medical purveyor, it may occasionally become necessary to purchase medical supplies. A special requisition is then made by the surgeon on a quartermaster, with the approval of the commanding officer. The quartermaster makes the purchase and furnishes the articles called for. The forms for this purpose are but rarely needed, and are not, therefore, reproduced in this place, but may be found in the Revised Regulations for the Army, Art. XLIV., Forms 2 and 3.

The special duty of the hospital steward in connection with these requisitions is to keep himself informed of the stock of medicines, dressings, and hospital stores on hand, and to notify the surgeon when the supply of any article—and especially of any important article—approaches exhaustion, in order that there may be time to replenish the stock by requisition before it is completely expended.

Besides this, it is frequently convenient for the hospital steward to make out the requisitions in accordance with the foregoing form, and carry them to the surgeon for his approval and signature.

SECTION II.—THE SUPPLY TABLE.

The medical supplies and their quantities are laid down in the standard supply tables, and not left to the discretion of individual surgeons.

The supply table contained in the "Revised Regulations for 1861," however, has been found in practice to present so many deficiencies and imperfections that it has been abandoned, and a new and carefully-prepared supply table substituted by order of the Surgeon-General.

When surgeons desire in any case, or for any special reasons, articles or quantities not laid down in this supply table, their requisitions, accompanied by the reasons therefor, must be sent to the Surgeon-General for his approval.

The revised supply table of 1862 has just been printed, and will be immediately distributed to medical officers.

SECTION III.—SEMI-ANNUAL RETURNS.

Medical officers in charge of medical supplies were directed, by Revised Regulations, to make duplicate returns of them annually to the Surgeon-General on the 31st of December. By a circular from the Surgeon-General's office, dated May 5, 1862, this has been modified, however, and the duplicate returns are to be made *semi-annually,* on June 30 and December 31, to the medical director of the military district in which they are serving, as well as to the Surgeon-General. Similar returns are also to be made by all medical officers when relieved from the duty to which their returns relate.

The returns must set forth the quantity of each article received, expended, and remaining on hand. They are also, under the head of Remarks, to show the condition of the stores, and particularly of the instruments, bedding, and furniture. The following is the form to be employed :—

Articles, and Characters or Quantities.		Return of Medicines, Instruments, Hospital Stores, Furniture, &c.
	On hand at last return.	
	Received since last return.	
	Total.	
	Expended with the sick.	
	Issued.	
	Lost or destroyed by unavoidable accident.	
	Worn out, or unfit for use.	
	Total expended, &c.	
	On hand.	
	Remarks.	

These returns are usually made out by the hospital steward in charge of the dispensary, and submitted to the surgeon for approval and signature. In order to make out the return correctly, the steward should keep in the dispensary a memorandum-book in which, from time to time, he should enter all articles lost or destroyed by unavoidable accident, and those worn out or unfit for service. The quantities on hand are to be determined by taking carefully an account of stock at the time of making the return; and, if the dispensary has been properly managed, the difference between the total quantity of each article expended, and the quantities returned as issued, lost, or destroyed, and worn out or unfit for service, will represent the quantity expended with the sick.

SECTION IV.—ARRANGEMENT OF THE DISPENSARY.

The various medicines, &c. kept in the dispensary must be arranged in some convenient order to facilitate dispensing. Every article should have its place, and should be kept in it except when actually in use.

The room selected for the dispensary should be dry, well lighted, and conveniently situated in relation to the other parts of the house. Where possible, water should be introduced by pipes, with a small sink and waste-pipe for the discharge of slops. Shelves should be put up adapted to the various sizes of the bottles and other original packages in which drugs are received from the purveyor, with a convenient number of drawers and closets.

A definite system should be kept in view in the arrangement of the stores upon the shelves and in the drawers and closets. Various plans of classification have been proposed: perhaps the most satisfactory is as follows:—

The several forms of preparations should be put together,—tinctures in one place, fluid extracts in another, extracts in a third, volatile oils in a fourth, and so on. The powerful alkaloids, morphia, strychnia, veratria, &c., should be kept carefully in a separate place, which should be secured with a lock and key.

The liquors kept in the dispensary should also be kept under lock and key.

The several articles of each class may be arranged alphabetically, or in such other order as is regarded as convenient. Where possible, it is best, as a general rule, to put the whole stock upon the shelves: by this plan only will it be possible to know readily what the stock on hand is, and when the supply of any article has been so nearly exhausted as to make it proper to require for more. Room may be made by putting the bottles several deep upon the shelves, taking care to put in the back rows bottles containing the same article only as those in front of them. Thus, for example, if there are a dozen bottles of tincture of opium, they may be arranged in three rows of four each, or, if the shelves are wide enough, in four rows of three each. One bottle only should be opened at a time, a second not being uncorked until the first is exhausted, when the empty bottle should be removed from the shelves and transferred to a closet specially assigned as a receptacle for empty bottles. To insure this, only one bottle at a time should have the original paper wrapper removed.

The same remarks apply to jars containing cerates, extracts, and so on.

The bottles and jars should be put upon the shelves, with the labels turned out, so that they may be seen at a glance.

The stock of liquors should not be kept in the dispensary, but in the room devoted to hospital stores,—a small supply, enough at the most for a few days only, being kept on hand in the liquor-closet of the dispensary.

Sponge, adhesive plaster, bandages, lint, muslin, and all similar articles, should be kept in separate drawers, each labelled with its contents.

The pestles and mortars, pill-tiles and pill-machines, spatulas, &c., should be kept in a closet or on shelves especially assigned to them. They should never be put away foul, but should invariably be cleansed thoroughly after using.

The dispensary should be furnished with a counter or table of convenient height, on which the scales and weights should be placed, and on which the various manipulations necessary in putting up prescriptions are performed.

The scales should be kept scrupulously clean and free from dust, as well as from stains and rust: otherwise all accuracy in weighing is impossible.

The water-faucet and the sink should be behind the counter.

No one should be allowed behind the counter but the steward in charge of the dispensary and his assistants.

All parts of the dispensary should be kept

scrupulously clean. The bottles and jars on the shelves should be dusted off with a feather brush daily, and from time to time they should be wiped with a damp cloth, as should also the shelf on which they stand. In performing this duty, the attendant executing it should begin at the topmost row of shelves, and, removing all the articles from one shelf at a time, should first wipe off the shelf, and, subsequently wiping off the bottles and jars, replace them each as it is cleansed in the same order as before. The steward in charge of the dispensary should have at least one assistant, whose duty it shall be to clean the pestles and mortars, pill-tiles, spatulas, &c. &c., keep the shelves and room clean, and make himself generally useful.

SECTION V.—CARE OF SURGICAL INSTRUMENTS.

Surgical instruments may be kept by the surgeon under his own personal care, but frequently, also, their care is intrusted to the steward in charge of the dispensary. The following precautions may be hinted:—

Surgical instruments should be invariably cleaned immediately after using. Tepid water answers very well for this purpose: hot water is injurious to the handles; with cold it is more difficult to remove dried blood. A little castile soap may be employed to get rid of the grease. After washing, they should be wiped perfectly dry, and, if stained, may be rubbed with a chamois-skin on which is placed a little rouge or tripoli. They should then be drawn a few times over a razor-strop, wiped with a clean chamois, and replaced in their cases.

Under no circumstances should more than a few hours be allowed to elapse, after using instruments, before they are cleansed. The proper time, however, when possible, is immediately after the surgeon has done with them.

When the edges become dull, the instruments may be honed in the following manner:—

A little oil being put upon the hone, the knife is taken in the right hand, while the hone is steadied with the left; the blade is laid obliquely, and, being held steadily at an angle of say thirty degrees, is drawn over the stone edge foremost, from heel to point, with a steady motion; the blade is then reversed, so as to bring the other side to the stone, and drawn back in the same manner, also, from heel to point.

This is repeated a number of times, until the requisite edge is obtained, when it is finished by drawing it a few times over a razor-strop. The character of the edge is determined by the angle at which the blade is held. If the angle is great, a blunt edge, suitable for cutting dense resisting structures, is obtained. If the angle is small, a fine, delicate edge, suitable for dissections of the soft parts, is given. The blade, however, should not be laid flat upon the stone, except in instruments where it has a back thick enough to give the proper angle. If, for example, a scalpel be sharpened by laying the blade flat upon the stone, the edge becomes too thin, and is liable to be bent or broken in use, constituting what is sometimes described as a wire edge.

Instruments not in use should be kept in their cases, the cases locked and covered by the gutta-percha or leather pouch in which it belongs. Once a month they should be examined, and any commencing rust be removed by the use of a little rouge or tripoli, as above directed. On the sea-coast, where the tendency to rust is great, it is advisable to smear the blades with a little mercurial ointment.

Instruments should be kept in a dry place,

under lock and key, and not allowed to be handled by any unauthorized person.

Care of the surgical instruments is especially necessary, not only because without it they soon become unfit for service, but also because it is directed that "these instruments will be accounted for to the Surgeon-General on the 31st day of December annually, in a special return, in which the true condition of each must be stated; and, if any be lost or damaged, a report of the facts and circumstances attending such loss or damage must be given."[*]

---

[*] Revised Reg., Art. XLIV. § 1304.

CHAPTER II.

Hints on Pharmacy for Hospital Stewards.

SECTION I.—REMARKS ON PRESCRIPTIONS.

UPON the steward in charge of the drugstore devolves the responsibility of compounding the prescriptions of the medical officers. The following brief remarks on this subject may perhaps, therefore, be found useful.

The prescription is headed with the name of the patient for whom it is intended. Then follows the list of ingredients and quantities, preceded by the character ℞, which is an abbreviation of the Latin word *recipe*, "take." The officinal names of the several ingredients are employed. The steward will, however, generally notice a difference between the termination of the officinal name and that of the name employed in the prescription. This is owing to the names being written in the Latin genitive case, the verb *recipe* governing the genitive.

Thus, the surgeon writes, ℞ Chloroformi ʒj, instead of "Chloroformum," which is the nominative, *chloroformi* being in the genitive case, and meaning "*of chloroform.*"

Thus, also, ℞ Zinci sulphatis grs. xx : Zinci sulphas being the nominative.

A still greater difficulty in the way of the steward occurs from the fact that surgeons very frequently abbreviate the officinal names for convenience, in writing their prescriptions, writing, for example, Hyd. chl. mit. for Hydrargyri chloridum mite; Potas. Iod., for Potassæ iodidum, &c. &c. As these abbreviations are, unfortunately, not always made in the same manner by different surgeons, a very long list of abbreviations might here be given, without exhausting the subject; and as it is directed in army regulations that no person shall be enlisted a hospital steward unless he is *sufficiently skilled in pharmacy* for the proper performance of his duties, it is presumed that such a list would be unnecessary here. Most of the abbreviations, moreover, at once explain themselves to any one familiar with the officinal names of the articles, as the steward should certainly be with those on the army supply table. The general rule may, however, be laid down, that the steward should under no circumstances allow himself to put up a prescription containing any abbreviation of the meaning of which he entertains the slightest doubt. In all such cases he should go at once to the surgeon for an explanation. By so doing, he not only avoids, at the time, mistakes which might be fatal, but gradually becomes thoroughly acquainted with all the abbreviations employed by the surgeon under whom he serves.

The quantities of the several ingredients employed are indicated by the usual symbols with Roman numerals affixed. Thus:—

Weights.
gr. a grain;
℈, a scruple;
ʒ, a drachm;
℥, an ounce;
℔, a pound.

Measures.
gtt. a drop;
♏, a minim;
fʒ, a fluidrachm;
f℥, a fluidounce;
O, a pint;
Cong. a gallon.

The Roman numerals follow these signs, thus:—ʒvj, i.e. six drachms; f℥xj, i.e. eleven fluidounces.

The following tables may be given for reference:—

Apothecaries' Weight.

Pounds.	Ounces.	Drachms.	Scruples.	Grains.
℔ 1 =	12 =	96 =	288 =	5760
	℥ 1 =	8 =	24 =	480
		ʒ 1 =	3 =	60
			℈ 1 =	gr. 20

THE HOSPITAL STEWARD'S MANUAL. 281

Avoirdupois Weight.

Pound.	Ounces.	Drachms.	Grains (Apothecaries').
lb 1 =	16 =	256 =	7000
	oz. 1 =	16 =	437.5
		dr. 1 =	27.34375

Weighing for prescriptions is always done in accordance with apothecaries' weight. Medical purveyors in the U.S. Army, however, are in the habit of employing, in the issue of medical stores, a pound which corresponds neither with the apothecaries' pound nor with that of avoirdupois weight. It is composed of sixteen ounces apothecaries' weight, and contains, therefore, 7680 grains,—being 1920 grains heavier than the apothecaries' pound, and 680 grains heavier than the avoirdupois pound.

Apothecaries' Measure.

Gallon.	Pints.	Fluidounces.	Fluidrachms.	Minims.
Cong. 1 =	8 =	128 =	1024 =	61440
	O. 1 =	16 =	128 =	7680
		f℥ 1 =	8 =	480
			f℈ 1 =	ℳ 60

The following remarks may be added with regard to certain domestic measures frequently alluded to in the administration of remedies.

A *teacup* is estimated to contain about four fluidounces or one gill. A *wineglass*, two fluidounces. A *tablespoon*, half a fluidounce. A *teaspoon*, a fluidrachm.

The steward may here be cautioned against the frequent mistake of identifying the drop with the minim. The minim is a fixed and unchangeable measure, which varies neither with the nature of the liquid nor the manner in which it is poured out. The drop, on the other hand, is exceedingly variable, differing in size considerably for different liquids, and even for the same liquid, in accordance with the shape of the bottle from which it is poured, and many other circumstances.

As an illustration of the variation caused by the nature of the liquid, it may be stated that in the experiments of Mr. E. Durand, of Philadelphia, on this subject, it was found that while 150 drops of sulphuric ether were necessary to make a fluidrachm, it required 132 of the tincture of the chloride of iron, 120 of aromatic sulphuric acid, 120 of laudanum, 78 of black drop, 57 of Fowler's solution, and but 45 of distilled water, for the same purpose.

The list of the articles and their quantities is followed in the prescription by short directions as to compounding it. These are generally written in Latin, and are frequently abbreviated. The following are the abbreviations most commonly employed :—

M.—Misce.—Mix.
Ft. pulv.—Fiat pulvis.—Make a powder.
Ft. pulv. xij.—Fiant pulveres xij.—Make twelve powders.
Ft. pulv. et divid. in chart. xij.—Fiat pulvis et divide in chartulas xij. } Make twelve powders.
Ft. pulv. in ch. xij. div.—Fiat pulvis in chartulas xij. dividenda.
Ft. ch. xij.—Fiant chartulæ xij.
Ft. solut.—Fiat solutio.—Make a solution.
Ft. inject.—Fiat injectio.—Make an injection (for urethra).
Ft. collyr.—Fiat collyrium.—Make an eye-wash.
Ft. enema.—Fiat enema.—Make an injection (for rectum).
Ft. mas.—Fiat massa.—Make a mass.
Ft. pil. xij.—Fiant pilulæ xij.
Ft. mas. in pil. xij. div.—Fiat massa in pilulas xij. dividenda. } Make twelve pills.
Ft. mas. et div. in pil. xij.—Fiat massa et divide in pilulas xij.
Ft. infus.—Fiat infusum.—Make an infusion.
Ft. haust.—Fiat haustus.—Make a draught.

Ft. garg.—Fiat gargarisma.—Make a gargle.
Ft. mist.—Fiat mistura.—Make a mixture.
Ft. emuls.—Fiat emulsio.—Make an emulsion.
Ft. ung.—Fiat unguentum.—Make an ointment.
Ft. linim.—Fiat linimentum.—Make a liniment.
Ft. troch. xxiv.—Fiant trochisci xxiv.—Make twenty-four lozenges.

After the directions as to compounding, follow those as to administration. These are always written in English, the direction being prefixed by the abbreviation *S.*—Signatura.

The directions are followed by the date and the signature of the medical officer.

The prescription, therefore, consists properly of three parts:—

1. The list of ingredients and quantities prefixed by the sign ℞.
2. The directions as to compounding,—generally a Latin abbreviation.
3. The directions for administration. These are preceded by the name of the patient, and followed by the date and the signature of the medical officer.

SECTION II.—COMPOUNDING AND DISTRIBUTION OF PRESCRIPTIONS.

Having read the prescription, the steward proceeds to compound it, varying his process according as it is a solution, a mixture, powders, or pills, &c., that he is to prepare.

Where the prescription consists of *liquids only*, they are measured seriatim in the graduated measure and poured into the phial which is to receive them, when the process is completed by corking and gently agitating the mixture.

In performing this duty, but one bottle should be taken down from the shelves at a time. The measure should be held by the thumb and finger of the left hand, and the stopper should be seized by the little finger of the same hand. The bottle is held in pouring with the right hand. The measure is held well up before the eye, so as to observe the quantity with accuracy; and, when it is obtained, the stopper is replaced, and the bottle put back in its place upon the shelf before proceeding to the next ingredient.

Where the ingredients of the prescription are partly solids and partly liquids, the quantities of the solids are to be determined by weight.

If the solids are saline or other soluble substances, and a solution is to be made, it is generally best to bruise them in a mortar with the liquids until their solution is effected, after which the product is transferred to a phial.

Where insoluble solid matters are to be suspended in the form of a mixture or emulsion, the mortar becomes still more important. The ingredients are to be rubbed steadily together until a smooth and uniform liquid is obtained, and the label of the phial into which the mixture is introduced should contain directions to shake well before administration.

When the prescription directs the preparation of any given number of *powders*, the ingredients in powder are carefully weighed out and thoroughly mixed together on a pill-tile with a spatula, or, preferably, in a mortar. The mixture having been completed, the product is to be divided into the number of equal parts called for by the prescription, the division being effected by the scales or the eye, according to the nature of the ingredients and the importance of accuracy. Each portion is then transferred to the paper in which it is to be folded. The papers for each set of powders should be neatly cut and of equal size. The folding is effected in the following manner. A crease is made by folding over the edge along the long side of the paper, at about one-third of an inch from the margin. The opposite edge is then laid in this crease, and the paper folded over longitudinally, so as to give the proper width. The ends are then folded over a spatula, to make the flaps of a proper width.

Uniformity in the size of the powders is exceedingly desirable. It may readily be attained by cutting out a small wooden gauge of the desired size, by which both the length and width of the powder may accurately be determined.

In the preparation of *Pills*, the materials for the whole number of pills, as directed by the prescription, are first to be weighed separately, then worked into a mass of the proper consistence, and afterwards divided into the number of pills called for.

To make a pill-mass where the ingredients are all dry powders, without increasing unnecessarily the size of the pills, requires often considerable ingenuity.

In the case of certain vegetable powders,

such as aloes, rhubarb, and opium, a mass suitable for rolling into pills may readily be formed by the aid merely of a small quantity of water, the powder being beat into a mass in a mortar during the gradual addition of the fluid.

Where, however, the powder is of an unadhesive character, as is the case, for example, with many vegetable powders and metallic salts, some adhesive ingredient must be added to them to enable a mass of pillular consistence to be formed.

Molasses answers an excellent purpose in very many cases. It must be added carefully, as an excess will make the pill-mass too fluid for manipulation. Gum arabic in small quantities may be added where the molasses does not give the mass sufficient cohesion. It is frequently used alone for this purpose, either in the form of powder or of thick mucilage, but is objectionable, as the pills produced by its use are apt to become excessively hard on drying.

For many vegetable powders castile soap answers very well, a small quantity readily imparting the necessary consistence. Resinous powders are particularly adapted to its use.

Where the prescription presents among its constituents one or more semi-solid extracts, it will frequently be found that these impart sufficient tenacity, and that by simply beating the ingredients together a suitable mass is obtained. But it sometimes happens, on the one hand, that the quantity of the soft extract is too small for the purpose, and then the addition of some such articles as those above enumerated becomes necessary; and, on the other hand, the extract may be of such quality and consistence as to make the mass entirely too soft to be rolled into pills. In the latter case the addition of some dry powder, which shall not interfere with the medicinal value of the prescription, becomes necessary. Powdered liquorice-root or wheat flour are well adapted for this purpose.

Where the materials to be made into pills are wholly semi-solid or liquid, the addition of some dry powder becomes yet more necessary. Wheat flour is very generally available, and is on the whole preferable to the crumb of bread, which is recommended by many pharmaceutists. Powdered liquorice-root, arrow-root, starch, and gum arabic are also used for the same purpose.

Other articles may be necessary in special cases, as, for example, magnesia in making pills out of balsam of copaiva.

Many other articles are used by pharmaceutists in giving elegance and consistence to pills. It is not, however, considered desirable to enumerate them in this place, because in most general hospitals treatises on pharmacy are accessible, and because those above mentioned comprise the chief that will be found accessible to the hospital steward in the field and at remote posts.

The pill-mass, having been properly formed, is next to be divided into the number of pills directed. This may be done either by a spatula upon a pill-tile, or with a pill-machine.

In the first case the pill-mass is rolled out upon the tile into a cylinder corresponding in length to the number of pills to be made, which is ascertained by measuring it upon a scale which is marked upon the surface of the tile. The rolling may be commenced with the hand and finished with the spatula. The cylinder is then cut by the spatula into equal pieces, one for each pill, in accordance with the same scale, which is generally ruled up to 18 or 24 pills. The pills are then finished by rolling them separately between the fingers or on the palm of the hand.

In general hospitals the steward is furnished with a pill-machine, by which pills may be made neatly with considerable rapidity. It consists of a smooth base-piece, in one part of which a number of parallel grooves (18 to 24) are made, and of a roller with a handle on each end, the back of which is smooth and the under surface grooved to correspond with the grooves in the base-piece. The pill-mass having been rolled on the smooth surface of the base-piece with the back of the roller until it is long enough to cover as many grooves as it is to make pills, the cutting surface of the grooves is adjusted, and by the motion of the roller the cylinder is at once divided into the requisite number of pills, which, if the operation has been properly conducted, will be so round as to require no further rolling.

The pills, having been completed either by hand or the machine, are, if very moist, to be spread out upon a sheet of paper with the edges turned up, or upon the bottom of a shallow box, to dry somewhat: they are finally introduced into a pill-box, if for dispensing, or into a bottle if made to keep on hand. In either case, some dry powder, such as starch, liquorice-root, or pulverized sugar, should be introduced to keep them from sticking together.

Where *ointments* and *cerates* are prescribed

containing several ingredients, they may very often be compounded upon the pill-tile by means of the spatula. Occasionally, however, the employment of heat is necessary to make the ingredients combine.

Cerate of Spanish flies may be spread for blisters by means of a spatula slightly warmed. Perhaps the best substance to spread it upon is ordinary adhesive plaster, spreading the cerate so that a margin of half an inch is left uncovered. This will serve to keep the blister in its place.

Plasters proper, usually require heat to spread them upon the prepared sheep-skin which is furnished for that purpose. The heat is best obtained by means of a hot iron of the proper shape (plaster-iron). Care must be taken not to heat the iron too hot, or the sheep-skin is shrivelled and the adhesiveness of the plaster diminished.

The prescription, having been put up, must not, whatever its nature, be allowed to leave the dispensary without a label. The labels usually employed in civil practice are not adapted to military hospitals, where the label should at once indicate whom the prescription is for, and give information to the nurse as to its administration, and to the surgeon as to its composition. The label must therefore be, in fact, a copy of the prescription, and should be made out in the following form:—

FOR PRIVATE JAMES SIMPSON,
WARD 2, BED 14.

℞—Pulveris opii, grs. vj.
Cupri sulphatis, grs. iv.
Ft. mas. in pil. xxiv div.
S. One pill to be taken every three hours.
2, 16, 1862.
....Surgeon, U.S.A.

This label should be written upon a neat slip of white paper, about two inches wide by five or six long. It may be pasted upon bottles if considered desirable; but, as the same bottles in a military hospital are to be used again and again, it will save labor in cleaning the bottles to tie the labels upon them. The corners of the label may be folded obliquely at one end, so as to form a point, and this may be tied to the neck of the phial by a thread. The label for pill-boxes may be secured in the same way to the bottom part of the box, leaving the lid free. For packages of powders or other packages, the label should be pasted upon the paper wrapper.

In putting up prescriptions, those for each ward should be put up together, attending to the wards *seriatim* in the order in which their prescription-books come to the dispensary in the morning. So soon as the prescriptions for any ward are complete, the chief nurse of the ward is to be notified, and will send an attendant to bring the medicines to the ward, where they will be distributed to the beds to which they belong, and administered strictly in accordance with directions.

PART V.

HINTS ON MINOR SURGERY AND DRESSINGS
FOR HOSPITAL STEWARDS.

CHAPTER I.

On Dressings.

SECTION I.—GENERAL PREPARATIONS FOR DRESSINGS.

To facilitate the dressing of wounds, it will generally be found convenient in hospitals to keep on hand one or more trays for dressings, which may be prepared in the following manner:—

A shallow box should be made, two feet long by eighteen inches wide and four inches deep, divided into equal halves by a partition which rises in the centre to the height of eight inches, and has an opening cut in it in such a manner as to serve for a handle.

In this box should be placed and kept constantly on hand the following articles, in quantities which will vary with the number of dressings to be performed daily in any particular hospital:—

Patent lint, neatly rolled; some charpie, or packed lint; an assortment of roller-bandages of various widths; adhesive plaster cut into strips three-fourths of an inch wide, also a roll uncut; isinglass plaster; two bundles of ligatures ten inches long, composed each of a single thickness of saddler's silk well waxed, and one of ligatures of two thicknesses twisted together, each bundle consisting of at least a dozen ligatures laid side by side, and surrounded for about half their length by a roll of paper fastened by a pin, so that the ligatures may be drawn out one at a time as wanted; a large pair of scissors; a sheet of patent lint eighteen inches square, neatly spread on one side with simple cerate; a pincushion amply provided with pins at one end, with from three to a dozen surgical needles ready-threaded at the other; a pocket-set of instruments; three to a dozen towels; and some sponges.

Besides this tray of dressings, basins with warm water, a bucket to receive soiled dressings, and a tin can filled with boiling water to heat the adhesive plaster, will be needed.

The surgeon who makes the dressings will generally need one attendant to carry the tray, and one for the basins and sponges, the bucket for soiled dressings, &c.

The attendant who carries the tray should

make himself thoroughly familiar with its contents and their respective places, and should be able at once to hand to the surgeon any article in it he may ask for, and to return it to its place when he has done with it.

The attendant who manages the sponges should keep constantly ready for the surgeon a clean basin of tepid water, with two or more well-soaked sponges, and as fast as one is soiled replace it with another, empty out the soiled water, and wash the soiled sponges, so as to be ready for the next patient, at the same time keeping an eye to the surgeon so as to hand him the can to heat adhesive plaster whenever he needs it.

SECTION II.—ON THE DRESSING OF WOUNDS.

In the army hospitals of the United States as at present organized, the dressings are usually made by the surgeons, assistant surgeons, and medical cadets, and comparatively seldom by the hospital stewards: no elaborate treatise on dressings is, therefore, required in this place. But as occasionally, and especially in the field and at remote posts, a certain portion of the dressings are necessarily made by the hospital steward, a few practical hints on the subject may be appropriate in this work.

The arrest of hemorrhage and the treatment of fractures, the introduction of sutures, and other steps requiring surgical skill and judgment, must, of course, receive the personal attention of a medical officer. The remarks here to be made are, therefore, limited to the dressings proper.

The dressing most generally found available for all wounds, whether incised, lacerated, gun-shot, or caused by surgical operations, is the water-dressing, either cold or warm, according to circumstances.

As a general rule, it may be said that cold-water dressings should be employed whenever the design of the application is to limit the degree of inflammation; warm-water dressings, where the design is to favor suppuration : at the same time, it should be understood that whenever the cold-water dressing is decidedly disagreeable to the patient, and especially when it causes shiverings or rigors, it should be at once discontinued and the warm-water dressing substituted.

The experience of our army surgeons is also in favor of dressings of the simplest kind, and opposed to all complicated systems of bandaging. The roller-bandage especially is liable to abuses, and should never be employed except in cases of fracture and where it is desirable to produce a certain degree of pressure.

The various complicated and beautiful bandages described and figured in the treatises on minor surgery will be found in practice, if applied to the treatment of wounds, to be not only troublesome and tedious, but in their results unclean, uncomfortable, and positively injurious.

The cold-water dressing as applied to a gunshot wound should consist simply of a small piece of lint folded double, saturated with cold water, and retained over the orifice of the wound by a couple of strips of isinglass or adhesive plaster. In incised or other wounds in which adhesive strips are necessary to retain the lips of the wound in apposition, the water-dressing may be applied above the strips and retained in the same manner. Usually no bandages of any kind are necessary.

Where a greater degree of cold is necessary, and especially where much inflammatory action is developed in the limb around the wound, *irrigation* should be resorted to. This is best effected by covering the parts to be irrigated with a double thickness of wet lint; cold water—ice-water, if desirable—is to be placed in a basin on a small table near the bedside; one or more strands of cotton lamp-wick are to be arranged with one end in the basin and the other laid upon the wet lint, or a strip or two of linen bandage may be used if lamp-wick cannot be obtained. By capillary action, a constant supply of cold water is taken up from the basin and deposited on the lint covering the limb. The limb should be placed on a piece of oiled silk or gutta-percha cloth so arranged that all the superfluous water may be drained into a bucket placed at the bedside.

This simple mode of irrigation is quite as good for most cases as any of the complex forms of apparatus designed for this purpose.

Where a greater degree of cold is necessary, a bladder may be filled with pounded ice and laid upon the parts. This, however, should never be done except by the express directions of the surgeon; and the greatest watchfulness and care should be employed to avoid freezing the surface.

The lint employed in these water dressings

should be changed at least once daily, or oftener in cases of profuse or offensive discharges.

Where the warm-water dressing is employed, it may be applied in the same manner as dressings of cold water; but it will here be found that it is convenient to cover the wet lint with a piece of oiled silk or gutta-percha cloth before applying the adhesive strips: by so doing, the warmth is much longer retained. Four or five thicknesses of lint saturated with warm water and thus covered will be found to retain warmth and moisture as long and efficiently as any poultice. Poultices are, moreover, uncleanly, disagreeable, and are very generally discarded by army surgeons in the treatment of wounds.

In healing wounds, when granulation is fairly under way and the suppuration is no longer profuse, lint spread with simple cerate, retained in place by adhesive strips, forms a simple and appropriate dressing. It is also a dressing frequently resorted to immediately after amputation and other operations, before suppuration has set in.

SECTION III.—OF THE ROLLER-BANDAGE AND ITS APPLICATIONS.

Although, as above remarked, the roller is to be avoided as much as possible in the treatment of ordinary wounds, yet it is very generally needed in dressing fractures, and may be required in many cases, as of chronic ulcers, &c., where a certain degree of pressure is desirable. A few remarks are, therefore, made on the roller and its application.

The roller-bandage is composed of a strip of muslin, usually one to four inches in width and three to seven yards in length. This is formed into a uniform and compact roll by beginning at one end and rolling it towards the other. Assorted roller-bandages of various widths and lengths, ready rolled, are furnished with the medical supplies of the army. Of late a very elegant article, rolled with the greatest precision by a steam apparatus, has been supplied.

Rollers may, however, be readily made, if not on hand, by tearing muslin into strips of the proper width and rolling them according to the following directions, which are also applicable in re-rolling bandages which have been used and washed.

To form a roller with the hands, begin at one end and fold the extremity upon itself several times, until a small cylinder of some solidity is obtained; then the ends of this cylinder are

held and it is revolved between the thumb and forefinger of the right hand, while the strip is passed smoothly between the thumb and forefinger of the left hand, in such a manner as to give a little tension. A good and uniform bandage can thus be made.

But in a large hospital, where many bandages are used, and where most of them are washed and re-rolled after using, the labor of making rollers in this manner would be far too great. A simple machine may in this case be constructed for the purpose by any carpenter, which will much facilitate the process. An axis of iron or strong wood (oak or hickory) is

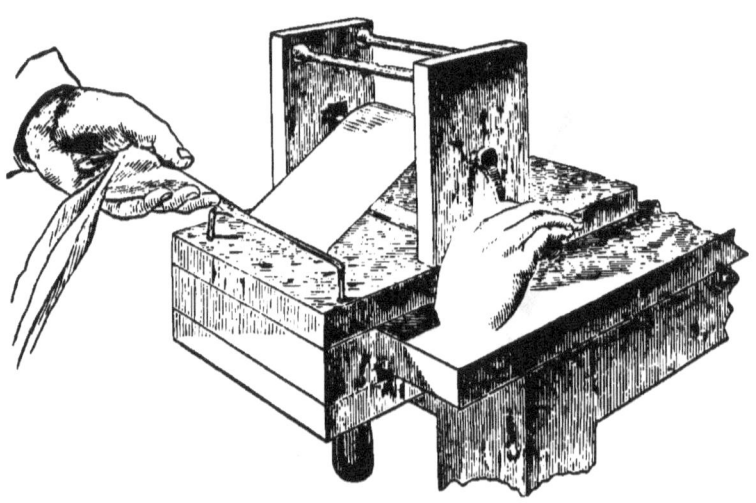

made eight or ten inches long, and about a quarter of an inch in diameter at its thickest end, with a slight taper towards the other extremity. At the thickest extremity is a handle to serve as a crank. This is to be passed through holes in two uprights, six or eight inches apart, set up in a square piece of board in such a manner that it can be readily made to revolve by the handle. One or more cross-pieces of wood or wire are so placed that the strip is smoothed by passing between them before it reaches the axis on which it is rolled. The figure explains itself. With such a machine a single attendant can roll a large number of bandages in a comparatively short time.

In applying the roller, the free extremity is laid with its external side next to the surface of the limb, where it is held by the fingers of the left hand until it is fixed by the subsequent turns, the bandage being gradually unrolled as it is applied by the right hand. When the dressing is completed, the extremity of the bandage is secured by a pin.

The roller receives various names, according to the mode of its application.

The *circular* bandage is formed by passing the roller circularly around the part so that each turn covers in nearly or completely that preceding it. This is also spoken of as "a few circular turns of the roller."

When the roller ascends the limb obliquely, each turn partly overlapping that which precedes, it is spoken of as the *spiral* bandage, or "spiral turns of the roller."

The most usual application, however, when a limb is to be covered in, is the *reversed bandage*, or "reversed turns of the roller." This is made as follows. The initial extremity of the bandage having been fixed by a few circular turns, the reverses are made as follows:—

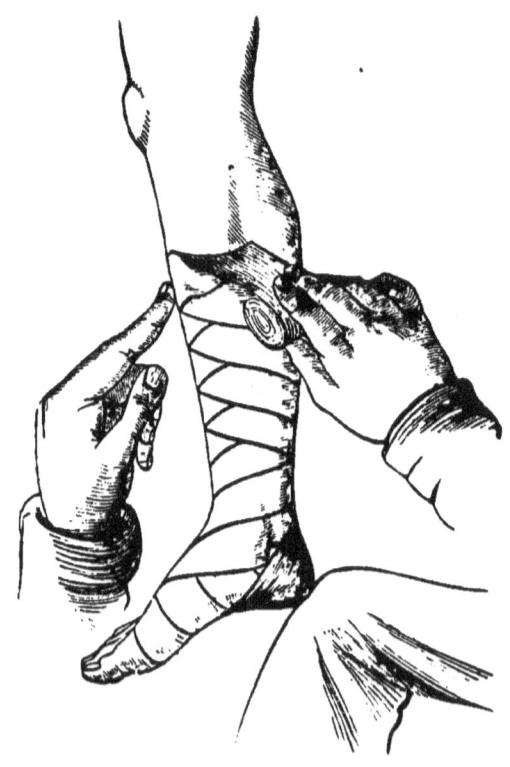

the upper edge of the bandage being fixed with two fingers of the left hand, the right, which has been holding the roller in the supine position, is to be pronated, and the bandage carried gently around the limb in this position until it reaches the corresponding point in the next turn, where the process is to be repeated; and so on up the limb. The figures will explain this process.

Two of the most frequently-employed and important applications of the reversed bandage are the spiral of the upper and the spiral of the lower extremities.

The spiral of the upper extremity requires a roller two and a half inches wide and seven or eight yards long.

It is applied as follows. Make a few circular turns around the wrist, beginning on the radial and passing towards the ulnar side; then carry the roller over the palm and back of the hand to reach the ends of the fingers, and ascend by simple spiral turns as far as the thumb. The ball of the thumb and wrist are then to be covered in by figure-of-8 turns, the forearm ascended by spiral reversed turns to the elbow, which is also to be covered in by figure-of-8 turns, and the arm ascended in the same manner as the forearm to the shoul-

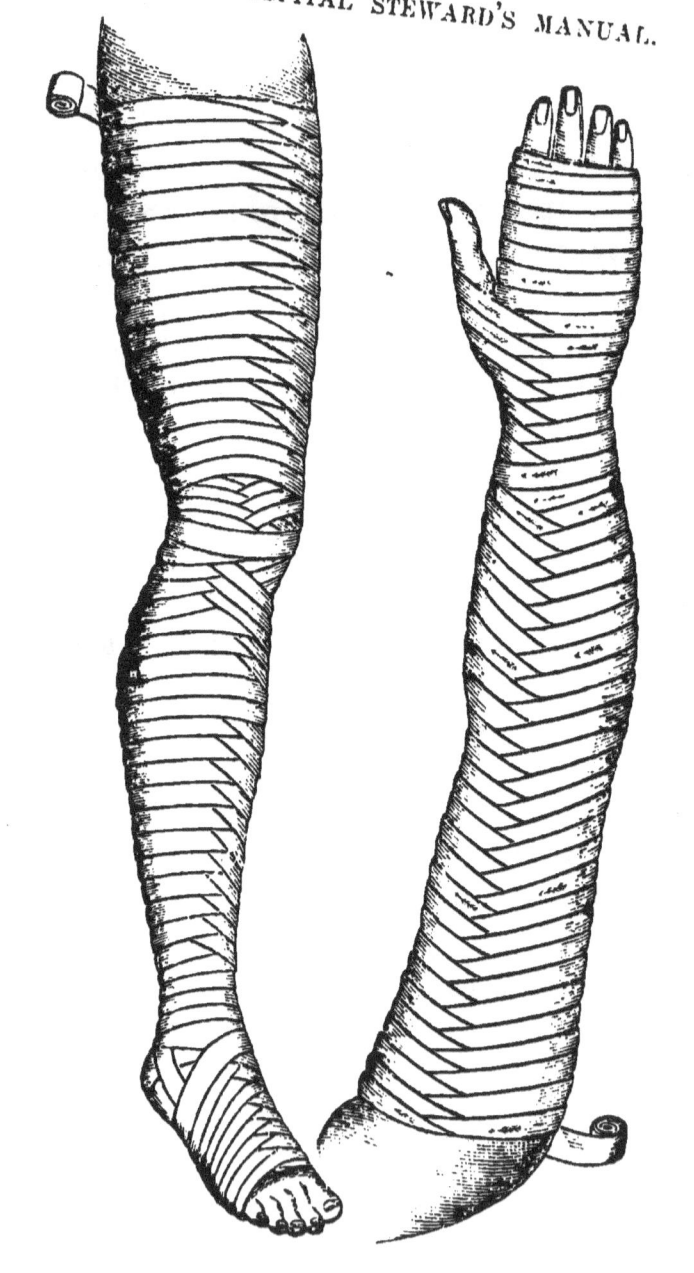

der, where the free end of the bandage may be secured by a pin. (See the figure).

The spiral of the lower extremity requires a bandage of the same dimensions, or perhaps half an inch wider, as that of the upper extremity.

Make a few circular turns around the ankle, beginning at the outer and passing towards the inner side; then, on reaching the internal malleolus, wind around it and over the tendo achillis, just above the heel, over the space between the external malleolus and the heel, and cross the sole of the foot to the great toe. Ascend by spiral turns from thence to the instep, from which wind around the inner side between the inner malleolus and the point of the heel, over the tendo achillis, to the outer side of the ankle above the malleolus, thence over the instep and point of the heel back to the instep, and make a figure-of-8 turn around the ankle, the instep, and the sole, after which ascend the leg by spiral reversed turns to the knee. (See figure).

If the knee and thigh are to be covered, take another roller, and, beginning below the knee, cover it in with figure-of-8 turns, and ascend the leg by spiral reversed turns to the groin.

Besides the roller-bandage, pieces of muslin of various sizes and shapes may be employed as bandages. The most generally available form is a square of muslin folded into a triangle or like a cravat. For detailed accounts of the application of these or other bandages, the hospital steward may consult "Sargent's Minor Surgery," which is now furnished with medical supplies to the army hospitals.

CHAPTER II.

Operations in Minor Surgery performed by the Hospital Steward.

SECTION I.—CUPPING.

By the term "cupping" is understood the application to the surface of the body, at convenient points, of one or more small cup-shaped vessels of glass or thin metal, from the cavities of which the air has been exhausted. Two methods are employed,—"dry cupping," or the application of "dry cups," and "wet cupping," or the application of "wet cups," called also sometimes "cut cups."

Dry cupping is effected by simply applying to the surface to be cupped the number of cups ordered, in such a manner as to produce a partial vacuum in the cavity of each, into which the integuments are forced by the atmospheric pressure without.

The manner in which this vacuum is produced will depend entirely upon the character of the cupping-apparatus furnished. Thus, it may be produced by a small air-pump made to fit upon the summit of each cup, in which is a small orifice furnished with a valve opening outward. Or it may be produced by a very ingenious apparatus recently brought into use, in which each cup has attached to its bottom a globe of India-rubber. This is simply compressed with the hand when the cup is applied, and then, the pressure of the hand being removed, the expansion of the globe by its elasticity to its natural form produces the necessary rarefaction of the included air.

The hospital steward, however, seldom has these more elegant methods of cupping at his command, the cupping-apparatus usually furnished to him, both in hospital and in the field, consisting simply of from six to a dozen plain cupping glasses or tins, and a scarificator.

The vacuum is created in these ordinary cupping glasses or tins by means of the heat generated by the combustion of alcohol. The inner surface of the cup may be moistened with alcohol, which is ignited, and, while still burning, applied to the skin; or a pellet of cotton or strip of paper, moistened with alcohol and ignited, may be dropped into the cup, which is to be applied while still burning. In either case, the flame is extinguished as soon as the cup is placed upon the skin, by the rapid abstraction of the oxygen of the contained air: so that there is no danger of burning the skin.

The object of "dry cups" is merely to produce congestion of the surface, with a certain degree of ecchymosis, that is, discoloration from blood effused in the integuments in consequence of the rupture of minute vessels during the process. Glass cups will, therefore, be found more useful when they can be obtained, because with them the degree of turgescence can readily be observed during the process.

Wet cupping requires, besides the congestion thus produced, that the congested surface should be incised in a number of places with a scarificator, and a certain flow of blood provoked from these incisions by a reapplication of the cups. In applying wet, or cut cups, therefore, the number prescribed are first to be applied in the same manner as in dry cupping, and then, after they have produced a certain amount of congestion,—say after five or ten minutes' application,—they are to be removed one at a time, the scarificator used, and the cups reapplied.

The scarificator is an instrument by means of which twelve to sixteen slight incisions can be made simultaneously, by as many little lancet-blades, over a surface about the size of the cup. It is furnished with a screw, by means of which the distance to which the lancet-blades protrude, and the consequent depth of the incisions, are regulated.

It is used by placing it upon the surface to be scarified, after having first set the blades back by pressing upon a lever made for that purpose, and then, touching the spring, all the incisions are instantly and neatly made.

The cup, having now been reapplied, is to be kept on until about an ounce of blood has flowed into it. And here again glass cups present advantages over those of metal, since with them the quantity of blood can readily be discerned, and the cup removed as soon as enough is taken.

Cut cups are, therefore, a method of local blood-letting.

The operation being completed and the cups all removed, the surface is to be cleansed from blood, and a piece of dry muslin, or, if there is much smarting, a cloth spread with simple cerate, applied.

When cupping is to be performed on the chest of thin persons, or upon the abdomen in cases of enteritis or peritonitis, it will be found that the previous application of a warm fomentation, or of a poultice, to the parts, will greatly diminish their sensibility and the pain of the operation.

SECTION II.—LEECHING.

Two kinds of leeches are employed in this country,—European and American. Neither of them are placed upon the supply table of the army. In certain situations, however, they are readily collected, and American leeches can be purchased in most localities at a moderate expense from the hospital fund.

In the application of leeches, the surface to which they are to be applied must first be prepared by washing it carefully with warm water. If the part is hairy, it should be shaved. To make the leeches take hold more readily, the parts on which it is designed for them to fasten may be moistened with sugar and water, or, still better, with blood drawn from the tip of the finger. The leeches are to be applied a few at a time, and as these take hold others added, until the whole number directed have fastened upon the part. As each fills, he lets go his hold and falls off; but if from any cause it is desired to remove them, or any of them, sooner, they may be made to let go their hold by putting common salt upon them. The leech should not be pulled off by violence, lest a portion of its head be broken off and remain in the wound, thus causing unnecessary irritation and killing the animal.

The American leech may be estimated as drawing about a drachm of blood, or even a little more: from six to eight will represent an ounce. The European leech is much larger, and may be estimated at two or three to the ounce of blood.

After the leeches are removed, bleeding may be encouraged, if so directed, by applications of warm water or of a warm poultice, or it may be checked, after carefully washing the part with cold water, by simple exposure to the air. Sometimes, however, the bleeding is quite profuse, and may resist this simple measure, in which case a sharp-pointed stick of nitrate of silver, introduced into the little bleeding orifices, will generally be found efficient.

Leeches may be kept on hand in good condition, for a long time, in tubs filled with water, at the bottom of which turf or peat is placed : the water should be changed about once a week. After they have been used, some means should be employed to evacuate the blood they have gorged: otherwise, they generally die. This may be done by sprinkling them with salt, or pouring salt water upon them, which causes them to eject the contents of their stomachs. A better plan, perhaps, is to make with a thumb-lancet two small punctures on the back of the leech, one on each side of the median line : through these the blood escapes, and the little wound subsequently heals. After using, leeches should be kept in a vessel separate from the others for two or three weeks, after which those which survive may be again employed.

SECTION III.—EXTRACTION OF TEETH.

For the extraction of teeth, a case of dental instruments is furnished with the medical supplies. This case contains a gum-lancet, forceps, a key, and an elevator.

The Gum-Lancet is used prior to grasping the tooth with the extracting instrument, for the purpose of separating the gum from the tooth.

Forceps of three shapes only are usually furnished,—one straight, for the incisors and cuspids; one curved, for the bicuspids and molars, and one with pointed blades, for the extraction of stumps.

The Key is usually furnished with two or three movable claws, so as to accommodate both sides of either jaw, and large as well as small teeth.

The Elevator is simply a lever with a sharp notched extremity, which is used in the extraction of stumps.

In the extraction of teeth by the forceps, the gum of the tooth to be removed is first well separated by means of the gum-lancet. Then the tooth is grasped by the forceps, taking care to apply the blades well down upon its neck, as near as possible to the alveolar process. The forceps are to be closed upon the tooth firmly enough to prevent them from slipping, but not with such force as to crush it,—a precaution especially to be attended to if it is much decayed. In the extraction of the incisors, the cuspids, and the bicuspids, a slight movement of rotation is now to be made, having for its object to loosen the tooth from its connections before exerting the traction which is to extract it. In the case of the molars, however, as rotation would be likely to break one or more of the fangs, a lateral, rocking motion is to be substituted.

The extraction of teeth by the key should not ordinarily be practised: it is a clumsy instrument, and is liable to break the teeth, bruise and lacerate the gum, and do other mischief. Occasionally, however, with the limited supply of dental instruments furnished to the hospital steward, its use may become necessary, especially in cases where the tooth is in such a state of decay as not to offer a good hold to the grasp of the forceps.

In the use of the key, the gum having been well separated, the claw is to be adjusted so that its point is well pressed down between the gum and the neck of the tooth; the handle of the key is then turned so as to bring the fulcrum against the gum on the opposite side, and the tooth grasped in this way is to be lifted perpendicularly, or nearly so, from its socket.

SECTION IV.—INJECTIONS.

Enemata, or injections by the rectum, may be directed by the surgeon not merely to procure the action of the bowels, but for various medicinal purposes.

The beak of the syringe or enema-pump should be warmed and well anointed with oil or lard. It should be gently and cautiously introduced, especially where the patient suffers from piles, or other diseases of the rectum; the fluid should be thrown in gradually and without violence, and, when the quantity directed has been introduced, a few moments should be permitted to elapse before the beak is withdrawn, lest on its too rapid removal the fluid, or a part of it, should escape with it.

A large syringe, made of hard India-rubber, is furnished with the medical supplies for this purpose. Where bulky enemata are directed, however, it will be found better to use the force-pump, which is furnished among the medical supplies with attachments by means of which it may be used either as a stomach-pump or for injection.

With this apparatus a steady and continuous stream may be thrown in. Printed directions for its use accompany the instrument.

The ordinary injection to procure the evacuation of the bowels consists of a tablespoonful of common salt and the same of molasses dissolved in a pint of warm water. This is what is generally understood when a patient is directed to have "an injection." The composition of any other enema must be specially directed by the surgeon.

Injections by the urethra are frequently employed, especially in cases of gonorrhœa. For this purpose, small syringes of hard India-rubber, or of glass, containing about half an ounce, are furnished with the medical supplies. The syringe being filled, its beak is to be oiled and introduced very gently into the urethra, and held in position by the thumb and last three fingers of the right hand, while the piston is pushed down by the right forefinger, the left hand being meanwhile employed in supporting the penis in position.

Various solutions are employed in this manner. None of them, however, should ever be resorted to except on the prescription of a medical officer. In any case, it will be generally found advisable to wash out the urethra by the use of a syringeful of lukewarm water, before throwing in the medicated solution.

THE END.

www.ingramcontent.com/pod-product-compliance
Lightning Source LLC
Chambersburg PA
CBHW030743230426
43667CB00007B/822